RANDOM
ACTS OF
KINDNESS
THEN & NOW

RANDOM ACTS OF KINDNESS
THEN & NOW

The Editors at Conari Press
with a new introduction by M. J. Ryan
and afterword by Addie Johnson

Conari Press

First published in 2013 by Conari Press
Red Wheel/Weiser, LLC
With offices at:
665 Third Street, Suite 400
San Francisco, CA 94107
www.redwheelweiser.com

ISBN: 978-1-57324-587-6

Library of Congress Cataloging-in-Publication data available upon request.

Cover design: *www.levandisgerdesign.com/BarbaraFisher*
Interior by Jane Hagaman

Printed in the United States of America
C
10 9   8 7 6 5 4 3 2 1

The paper used in this publication meets the minimum requirements of the American National Standard for Information Sciences—Permanence of Paper for Printed Library Materials Z39.48-1992 (R1997).

For Anne Herbert,

the woman who started the movement

CONTENTS

Carry out a random act of kindness, with no expectation of reward, safe in the knowledge that one day someone might do the same for you.

—Princess Diana

INTRODUCTION

It would not be an overstatement to say that publishing *Random Acts of Kindness* twenty years ago changed my life. As one of the publishers of Conari Press at the time, I had no idea of the outpouring of stories and publicity that one little book could generate. Suddenly I was one of the spokespersons for the book and the movement that it birthed. I was on the radio, on TV, at speaking engagements large and small. The movement swelled around us. Our four-person office was inundated with mail (believe it or not, this was in the dinosaur days before email and social media) as thousands of people, young and old, wrote in to share their stories. I will never forget the letter from the high school senior who told me that he'd been suicidal until he read the book and decided that life was worth living. Talk about a positive effect! We ended up creating a non-profit Random Acts of Kindness Foundation to support school and community involvement in the movement which had 300-plus active participating "chapters" and around 90,000 active participants. An international World Kindness Movement also sprouted, which is still going strong with eighteen participating countries from Canada to Singapore.

Because I didn't want to be a hypocrite in my role as spokesperson, I began to intentionally practice random acts of kindness on a daily basis. And, low and behold, something amazing happened to me. Like the suicidal high schooler, I got happier. *A lot* happier. Rather than being the mildly depressed person I'd been for almost forty years, I was suddenly Susie Sunshine. I felt less worried and more content with my life. The world seemed a much friendlier place. And while I can't guarantee that if you do good to strangers you'll become a millionaire, I must report that my life got easier. Much easier. Today, two decades later, I am still amazed at the power of such a small thing to create such uplift.

I get the same uplift from reading the stories in this book. Like you, I am busy. Very busy, too busy, but of course, like you, I have to keep moving to keep up. Next on the list: write the introduction to *Random Acts of Kindness Then & Now*. Okay, open the file and read the stories. I begin to read. Suddenly my heart softens and warms. Life feels worth living as I remember to enjoy my moments rather than just race through them. What is it about these acts of kindness that are so powerful?

This question has, in many ways, directed my career as a writer. I became fascinated with discovering the other simple things we can do on a daily basis to improve our mood and our connections with other people. And I became obsessed with finding out why these small actions make such a big difference in our happiness. The search led me through the world's wisdom traditions and the emerging field of positive psychology as well as the exploding arena of neuroscience.

I won't bore you with a discussion of obscure brain areas, but I do want to give you some highlights I discovered in my journey that you will hopefully find as fascinating and useful as I do.

From a spiritual perspective, I've come to understand that the reason we feel happy when we're kind is because we experience something rarely spoken of in Western culture. (I've read over fifty books on happiness and only one mentions it!) Buddhists call it *mudita*—sympathetic joy. The upswelling of the heart at the happiness of someone else.

Sympathetic joy is the opposite of envy. It's one of the reasons why a random act of kindness feels so good. We experience in ourselves the good feelings of the other person. Actually the giver gets a double whammy of happiness—anticipatory joy in thinking of how the person is going to feel, as well as the actual moment when he or she receives the benefit of our action. Sympathetic joy is such a wonderful feeling that you don't even have to be there when the person receives the gift to feel great. Just thinking about how the person is going to feel when they realize you put a quarter in their expired parking meter gives you a bolt of pleasure.

From a psychological viewpoint, positive psychologists have shown that acts of kindness do boost mood. A few years ago, Stanford University psychologist Sonja Lyubomirsky asked students to carry out five weekly random acts of kindness. Her results? The students reported higher levels of happiness than a control group, with those who did all five acts of kindness in one day per week reaping the biggest rewards by the end of the six weeks.

Another researcher, Barbara Fredrickson, discovered that if you count the number of times you're kind in a day, you get happier. She's also demonstrated that kindness and other positive emotions actually help us reduce the stress response and recover from the negative emotions—anger, worry, fear, pessimism. And in her book *Positivity,* Fredrickson explains that experiencing positive emotions like kindness in a 3-to-1 ratio with negative ones leads people to a tipping point beyond which they naturally become more resilient to adversity and effortlessly achieve what they once could only imagine. This certainly has been true in my life.

Finally, psychologist Jonathan Haidt found that watching acts of kindness created physical sensations, such as a warm, pleasant, or tingling feeling, and that people who watched compassionate and kind acts wanted to help others and become better people themselves.

Have you ever been with someone who, when they do you a courtesy and you offer thanks, says, "My pleasure?" It truly is a pleasure to spread kindness, even if it's simply holding the door for someone who is struggling with a load of packages. It turns out that when we do nice things for other people—random or otherwise—we activate a part of our brain that plays an important role in experiencing pleasure, the same part of the pleasure circuit that's activated by exercise. (My brain must be wired differently, though—kindness always feels good, but exercise—never!)

So what does this all mean? Not only will reading the stories in this book make you feel happy, but it will likely spur you to action. If you want to get the full benefits, do five random acts of kindness a week and write them down. Beyond an uptick in mood in the moment and an increase in positivity in general, I predict you'll have another positive experience. In the great wheel of interconnection, you'll get to see how being kind to someone else is really being kind to yourself.

I was reminded of this through the story of the person who stopped to help someone change a flat tire and then ten minutes later, got a flat himself. Guess who stopped to help? Yup, the person he'd just helped. So if you need yet another reason to become a kindness angel, here it is: what you do will most likely come back to you, hopefully tenfold.

May kindness continue to grow in our hearts and in the world,

—M. J. Ryan

ROADSIDE ANGELS

STORIES OF KINDNESS
FROM THE ROAD
AND ABROAD

*The smallest act of kindness is worth more
than the grandest intention.*

—Oscar Wilde

A Hundred-Dollar Bill

I arrived at the airport in Pullman, Washington, excited about my approaching interview for admission to the University of Washington's veterinary school. I went directly to the rental car agency to pick up my car, only to find, to my disbelief and horror, that my credit card had been declined and I had no other means of payment.

I ran to the pay phone and called my roommate back in California. I was trying to explain what had happened in between hysterical sobs, when a man walked up to me, tapped me on the shoulder, handed me a one hundred-dollar bill, and walked away. Thanks to the generous compassion of a total stranger I made the interview on time and was accepted into the veterinary school.

A MISSED BUS

One year when I was away at school I had gone to the Greyhound bus depot to catch a bus home for Christmas break. I looked all over for the right bus, but none of the buses lined up at the terminal had my destination on them. As I was standing there trying to figure out where my bus was, one pulled out and the driver changed the sign as he was leaving—to exactly where I wanted to go. I stood there watching my bus disappear down the highway; I must have been visibly upset because a woman came over, took my arm, and led me to the street. She hailed a taxicab, gave the driver a five-dollar bill, and told him to get me over to the ferry dock quickly, because the bus made a stop there before heading out onto the highway. She wished me a Merry Christmas, and all I could do was smile.

* * *

No one is useless in this world who lightens the burdens of another.

—Charles Dickens

Ah, Bambini!

My husband and I were traveling in Italy with two small babies and an au pair. We would trade sightseeing time with the au pair so we could all visit the requisite churches and museums. But on this day we took the babies along, since we only had one day to go to Assisi and all of us urgently wanted to see it. The morning was wonderful—feeling like happy pilgrims, we read each other stories of St. Francis while the babies cooed and gurgled as we drove up the winding streets.

But by the end of a very hot day traipsing up and down hills in the ninety-degree Italian sun, the kids were crying nonstop. One was throwing up; the other had diarrhea. We were all irritable and exhausted, and we had a three-hour trip ahead of us to get back to Florence, where we were staying. Somewhere on the plains of Perugia we stopped at a little trattoria to have dinner.

Embarrassed at our bedraggled state and our smelly, noisy children, we sheepishly tried to sneak into the dining room, hoping we could silence the children long enough to order before they threw us out. The proprietor took one look at us, muttered "You wait-a here," and went back to the kitchen. We thought perhaps we should leave right then, but before we could decide what to do, he reappeared with his wife and teenage daughter. Crossing the dining room beaming, the two women threw out their arms, cried, "Ah, bambini!" and took the children from our arms, motioning us to sit at a quiet corner table. For the duration of a long and hospitable dinner, they walked the babies back and forth in the back of the dining room, cooing, laughing, and singing them to sleep in gentle, musical Italian. The proprietor even insisted we stay and have an extra glass of wine after the babies were asleep! Any parent who has reached the end of his or her rope with an infant will agree that God had indeed sent us angels that day.

. . . .

If you want happiness for an hour—take a nap.
If you want happiness for a day—go fishing.
If you want happiness for a month—get married.
If you want happiness for a year—inherit a fortune.
*If you want happiness for a lifetime—help someone
    else.*

—Chinese proverb

Two Flat Tires

I used to make an eighty-mile drive to visit my parents, and there's a forty-mile stretch of the road that's in the middle of nowhere. One day as I was driving alone along this barren patch, I saw a family on the side of the road with a flat tire. Normally I do not stop in such situations, but for some reason I felt the need to do so that day. The family was very relieved when I volunteered to drive them to a gas station about ten miles down the road to get help. I left them at the station because the attendant said he would take them back to their car and drove on my way. About twelve miles later, I had a blowout. Since I couldn't change the tire myself, I was stranded and not sure what to do. But in only about ten minutes a car came along and pulled over to offer help. It was the same family I had stopped for earlier that day!

We realize that what we are accomplishing is a drop in the ocean.

But if this drop were not in the ocean, it would be missed.

—Mother Teresa

I think it pisses God off if you walk by the color purple in a field somewhere and don't notice it.

—Alice Walker

THE CARPET SELLERS OF KATHMANDU

After a trek to Mount Everest, I found myself in a rug shop in Kathmandu considering buying a carpet.

I had entered to big smiles and choruses of "Welcome, my sister!" from the proprietors, a pair of brothers from Kashmir named Qayoom and Yousef. After introductions and handshaking all around, I was offered a seat and something to drink. At first I declined, but Qayoom insisted, so I asked for black tea. He said something in a language I couldn't recognize to an old man with half-closed eyes who stepped outside to fetch our drinks.

Qayoom lived with Yousef's family in four rented rooms in a quiet section of town. The old man lived with them. They had found him drunk and living on the streets, and, as good Muslims, they felt it was their duty to help. So they offered him a job on the condition that he quit or at least cut back. The old man took a new name, Surkedai, which translates to "Happy Man." He used to be "one hundred percent bad" when it came to alcohol, said Yousef. Now he is "eighty percent good and only twenty percent bad." In return Surkedai fetches drinks for customers, dusts the shelves of small knickknacks in the front room of the shop, walks the twenty minutes back to the house to bring lunch each day, and re-rolls the carpets that customers aren't interested in.

This old man, whose wife and family abandoned him to the gutter because of his drinking problem, now has a place to sleep, a small wage, and people who care about him.

Un-lost

I was wandering aimlessly through the aisles of the Sears automotive department in a big, impersonal East Coast city. I felt terribly alone, far from home, and so totally preoccupied with my own misery and loneliness that I don't think I really saw anything on the shelves. After awhile I became aware of a small child about three or four years old, walking and crying at my side. I don't know how long she had been keeping me company, but I sensed that somehow she had gravitated toward me as someone who would help her. I knelt beside her and asked if she was lost; with tears streaming from her eyes, she just nodded. I held out my hand and told her not to worry, that we would find her parents. She put her hand in mine and I led her up to the counter, where two wonderful salesladies immediately enveloped her and promised to find her parents.

As I was leaving the store I heard the announcement over the paging system and had no doubt that she would soon be reunited with her parents. I also realized that all my own doom and gloom had disappeared. I thought to myself that just as that little girl had renewed my spirit, perhaps the small acts of strangers willing to help would allow this child to grow up with a little less fear and a more compassionate outlook on the world.

The ocean, king of mountains, and the mighty
*   continents*

Are not heavy burdens to bear when compared

To the burden of not repaying the world's kindness.

—Buddha

It is good to have an end to journey toward; but it is
the journey that matters, in the end.

—Ursula K. Le Guin

IN A STRANGE TOWN

On my first trip to the States, I arrived in New York as a student and went down to the bus station to buy a ticket. I had my money in one hand and my handbag in the other—it didn't have anything valuable but my address book in it. Going up to the counter to pay, I put my bag down for a second and when I looked again, it was gone. I couldn't believe it. I started to panic because I realized that without my address book I didn't know how to get in contact with my brother, who I was going to stay with.

The friend who was with me suggested we go to the police. With what I knew about New York's reputation I told her that would be a waste of time. But we went anyway and met two policemen who seemed to be straight out of a television show. They couldn't have been nicer. They said, "Such a terrible thing to happen to you on your first trip to America." They took down the details and then started asking me questions: Where was I going? Did I know how to get in touch with my brother? Of course I didn't, because my address book was gone. Then one policeman said, "Do you know anybody who knows him?" And I remembered I knew his in-laws. So they allowed me to make a long-distance phone call to the in-laws to get my brother's address and phone number. And when I got off the phone they said I should go ahead and call my brother right then and there so I wouldn't be anxious. Then they walked us back to the bus stop where we could find our way back to our hotel.

THE TAXI DRIVER

New York City is a great place to find kindness because it is always such a surprise. I was going to a trade show and my plane was delayed, so by the time I got to my hotel everyone I was supposed to meet had already left for the show. The concierge told me that if I walked around the block I could catch a shuttle. So I walked to the bus stop, but the last shuttle had already gone. Then a young man standing on the sidewalk said, "The convention center isn't very far, it's only four blocks." So I started walking. But it wasn't only four blocks, and I walked and walked.

It started getting dark, I was already an hour late for my meeting, and I found myself in the warehouse district— definitely not the kind of place you want to be in when you're all by yourself in New York. Eventually I saw a little light in the distance and started walking toward it. As I walked, a taxi drove past, then backed up and asked me where I was going. I told him and he said, "Get in. I'll take you there." By then I was really relieved, particularly when it turned out to be quite far to the convention center. To make the moment even sweeter, when the driver dropped me off—safely back among my friends—he wouldn't take any money from me.

In Need of a Guide

I had been traveling in Asia for three months and was in Hong Kong to meet up with my boyfriend who was flying in for a week. Somehow his pending arrival had brought up all the homesickness that had stayed buried during the day-to-day difficulties and joys of traveling. I had boarded a bus that I thought was going to the airport, but the bus flew past the airport without stopping and I burst into tears. I was eager to meet my boyfriend's flight but instead I was on a bus to God knows where. I kept calling out "airport, airport," but the bus driver spoke no English.

A Chinese woman who spoke some English told me to get off at the next stop, which was in the middle of an expressway. The woman exited and headed off in the opposite direction, after indicating that I was to follow a second woman who was gesturing wildly and speaking Chinese. Then she too turned off in a different direction after aiming me down still another street. After a few steps I noticed an old man who had been there all along. Quietly and patiently, looking back every so often to make sure I didn't get lost, he guided me through the crowded and confusing streets of Kowloon to the airport. To this day I think gratefully of my shy and silent guide and of course his more vocal friends.

TAKE MY SEAT

I was standing in line getting ready to board a plane when this guy comes rushing up to the ticket counter. He had obviously sprinted through the terminal and was furious when the woman at the counter told him his reservation had been cleared and his seat given away. She offered to get him a confirmed seat on the next flight, which unfortunately was not leaving for nearly five hours, but he would have none of it. He started screaming about how important it was that he get to Chicago by seven, how irresponsible the airline was when, after all, he had a confirmed ticket, how he wanted to see the supervisor, and on and on and on.

Finally he stopped his tirade and, in a very quiet voice, said, "I'm really sorry. I'm just completely stressed out and I can't believe I am going to miss this meeting." Right then an old man who was standing in front of me in the boarding line watching this whole thing stepped up to the counter and said, "Here, take my seat. I'm retired and I'm in no real hurry to get anywhere." The guy was so happy and so humbled at the same time that it looked like he was going to cry. Then he took the ticket and got on the plane.

Life's most persistent and urgent question is, What are you doing for others?

—Martin Luther King, Jr.

Let a good person do good deeds with the same zeal that an evil person does bad ones.

—Shalom Rokeach

ROADSIDE

We were on vacation in Florida, with four kids all under the age of ten. The weather had been very hot and humid so this particular day we decided to pack a cooler full of sandwiches and soft drinks and drive out along the coast until we found a nice beach. It was sort of an adventure since we really didn't know where we were going, but after a while we found a beautiful beach that was pretty isolated. We parked and unloaded ourselves onto the sand. It was really great, except after a few hours it got too hot for the kids and they were starting to whine and complain. So we decided to head back to the air-conditioned hotel.

When we got back to the car we discovered the keys, dangling from the ignition with all the windows rolled up and all the doors locked. In frustration I screamed, "Who locked the doors?" to which Beth, my five year old, responded, "You tell us always to lock the doors." I felt totally defeated. At first I was just going to smash the window in, but after Beth's evenhanded comment, I thought that would be a bit too violent. So I walked up the road about a half-mile to a house along the beach. I knocked on the door, and an elderly couple invited me in. They let me use their telephone to call roadside service, then packed me into their car and drove back to pick up the rest of my family. They brought us all back to their home, and within a few minutes the kids were swimming in their pool while my wife and I sat on an air-conditioned veranda sipping a cool drink and swapping vacation stories. Roadside service came and went, and three hours later we headed back to our hotel, refreshed and glowing from the surprising and wonderful experience.

....

Past the seeker as he prayed, came the crippled and the beggar and the beaten. And seeing them, the holy one went down into deep prayer and cried, "Great God, how is it that a loving creator can see such things and yet do nothing about them?"

And out of the long silence, God said, "I did do something. I made you."

—Sufi teaching story

CHOSEN PEOPLE

An adventurous group of Australians traveled to Nepal to attempt to climb Mt. Everest. At the 10,000-foot level, one member of the group became very sick with chills, fever, nausea, and vomiting. His "friends" wrapped him up in his sleeping bag and continued their climb. Two weeks later, he woke up in a Sherpa village. They had found him on the mountainside, where he had slipped into a coma, and had brought him to their village to nurse him back to health.

It took many months for the climber to fully regain his health. Finally, six months after being abandoned on the mountainside, he returned to the Australian embassy in Kathmandu to find that his passport had been turned in by his climbing partners with the explanation that he had died on the slopes of Mt. Everest.

The man who had been so lovingly nursed back to health was—in his life in Australia—a trained nurse. He had his worldly possessions shipped from Australia to Nepal, and he returned to the Sherpas to repay their kindness by living, working, and caring for his new "chosen people."

A Trip to the Post Office

Kindness is not always a straight line. I was traveling in Central America with a friend, and we were looking for a post office. We were standing on the corner and did not know what the Spanish word for "post office" was. Some kind soul could see we were confused and came up to us. We tried to explain what we were looking for, and he said, "Oh yea, yea," and led us, with our backpacks on in the middle of the heat of the day, down all these little crooked streets. It seemed like we walked for miles. Finally, he pointed us toward a building without any name on it. But when we went in, it turned out not to be the post office.

When we came out and were again standing around looking lost, someone else came up and asked if she could help—she knew where the post office was. Again we headed off as she guided us to another building which also had no sign and which also turned out not to be the post office.

At this point we decided that even though we didn't know where we were, we were not going to listen to anybody else. But then another person came up and said, "I can help you." We said no thank you, but he was very insistent. He actually grabbed me by the hand and dragged me through the streets. Circling around, we came back to the original corner we had been standing on when we began. The stranger pointed across the street, and there was the post office.

THE HILLS OF SAN FRANCISCO

You hear stories all the time about tourists trying to drive in San Francisco. I discovered a whole new twist one day when I was walking up a particularly steep hill and saw a car stopped near the top with a very frightened woman inside. As I watched, she made a few attempts to get moving but each time seemed to lose more ground than she'd gained. Then a man came out of the corner market. The next thing I know, she gets out of the car and goes around to the passenger side while he climbs into the driver's seat and promptly drives the car up over the top of the dreaded hill. By then, I had reached the store where the helpful man's wife was standing, watching the proceedings. She told me that her husband, who owns the market, has been doing that for years, and that during the summertime— peak tourist season—he will "rescue" as many as ten scared drivers a week.

MOTORCYCLE ANGELS

In 1972 I was living in Utah, and my sister and I took a drive down to the Great Salt Lake—miles away from anything. When we got back to the car in the evening we noticed a very flat tire. We were both in our early twenties and had no idea how to fix it. While we were standing there wondering what to do, a gang of ten guys on motorcycles roared over the rise and pulled to a halt right in front of us. We were scared to death—after all, we had watched enough television to know that this was not a good situation.

The leader of the group got off his bike, followed by three other big, burly, rough-looking men. He looked straight at us and said, "Gimme your keys." With a sinking feeling of hopelessness, my sister handed them over. The four men then proceeded to change our tire while we watched. Then the leader came back, handed us the keys, and said, "Now go home." They roared off into the sunset, and ever since that day I am very careful not to judge people by how they look.

LOST AND FOUND

My girlfriend and I are avid backpackers. In my mind it is such a different reality once we are on the trail, and I guess that is why I always put all of my worldly things in a small green bag and stuff it away in a corner of my backpack. I mean everything—my wallet, with all my ID, credit cards, license, etc., all my money, my keys—everything you need to survive in the modern world but is irrelevant in the woods.

This particular trip was a five-day trek through some of the most beautiful parts of the Cascades. As we headed back down to the car, I was really sad to be leaving such a simple and beautiful way of living. I could just feel the tension and anxiety beginning to creep back into my body as we got closer and closer to civilization. When we finally got to the car there was a small piece of paper tucked under the windshield-wiper blade that read, "left rear tire." I walked back and looked at the left rear tire, but it was fine. The note made no sense to me at all—three seconds back into the world, and already lunacy. Then I started fishing through my backpack for my green bag. It wasn't there. I looked back at the left rear tire—there was the bag. I have no idea when I lost it, who found it, or how they ever found my car amid all the possible parking places. My keys, my wallet, nearly $100 in cash, all neatly tucked in my zip-up green bag sitting on top of my left rear tire. Thank you, whoever you are. You gave me back much more than you know.

However big Tigger seemed to be, remember he wanted as much kindness as Roo.

—A.A. Milne, *The House at Pooh Corner*

FUGITIVES ABROAD

When we were in our early twenties, my best friend and I spent six months traveling throughout Europe. We had bought train tickets in Italy to go to Greece via Yugoslavia. Once on board the government-run train, a pair of Yugoslav soldiers entered our compartment to collect our tickets. The blond one, who seemed to be the one in charge, immediately became abusive. Though they spoke no English, I managed to communicate through the dark-haired soldier, who spoke broken French. Apparently our tickets were insufficient to get us to Greece, and the blond soldier demanded money on the spot. Unsure whether our tickets really were inadequate or if this was simply an extortion attempt, we swore we had no money on us. The blond soldier then proceeded to confiscate our passports and lock us in our compartment, where we stayed for two days and nights with only a little water and some chocolate.

Soldiers barged into our compartment around the clock, often with dogs, always with guns, each time asking for our identification, as if they didn't already know who we were. The blond was usually among them and he was always gruff and intimidating, often leering at my friend. We saw the dark-haired interpreter a few times, but he rarely spoke. Eventually the blond soldier said we would not be able to leave the country and that we would be turned over to the Yugoslav police.

As we approached the border, pondering our predicament and wondering if we should reveal to them our $500 in travelers' checks, the dark-haired soldier suddenly slipped into our compartment and motioned us toward the back of the car. As our train came to a halt at the checkpoint, he pointed to a local train on the next track. As we jumped to the ground, he quickly handed us our passports, three apples, and two tickets to the first Greek town over the border. Then he was gone.

....

I believe that man will not merely endure; he will prevail.

He is immortal, not because he alone among the creatures

has an inexhaustible voice, but because he has a soul,

a spirit capable of kindness and compassion.

—William Faulkner

A Friend in a Big City

Some years ago my daughter and I were living in Germany. We got word that some of her stateside friends were coming on a trip to Paris and the Loire Valley. We arranged to meet them in Paris, and after an exciting eight-hour train ride, we hooked up and had a fantastic time.

On the final day of their visit, we ended up on a tour bus, dropping them all off at the airport with many tears and hugs, filled with the joy of the time we had spent together. My daughter and I, however, still had to get to the train station all the way across Paris to catch our train. We had originally arranged with the tour bus driver to drop us off at the first subway station, but everything that day seemed to take twice as long as we thought it would; we started worrying about making our train, especially now that our baggage was so heavy with treasures.

If we missed the train, we would miss all our connections and not make it home in time for work and school the next day. Our bus driver Ahmed spoke very little English, but he must have seen that we were worried, because we sailed right past the Metro station and he drove us through the unbelievable mess of Parisian rush-hour traffic, delivering us to the front entrance of the train station with plenty of time to spare. He wouldn't even accept the extra money we offered him, only wishing us a safe journey. In a city with a reputation for being brusque and impersonal. it was such a heartwarming act of kindness.

SCOTCH TAPE TO THE RESCUE

Some years ago, I was driving home alone in my Volkswagen beetle when the car suddenly lost power. I coasted to a stop on the shoulder, got out, and saw only cornfields for miles in every direction. After a while a car pulled over and a man got out and asked in a thick Irish brogue, "Would you be needin' help?" I quickly explained to him what had happened and he said, "I'll have a look, shall I?"

All hope of rescue died as he opened the hood to find no engine. I explained that the engine was in the back, and without missing a beat he shifted position and tinkered around for a few minutes. Then his head popped up and he said, "I've just what's needed." He returned to his car, and brought back a roll of Scotch tape. I just stood there in disbelief as he dived back into the engine compartment to apply his magic remedy.

"Start 'er up," he said. I complied, and the engine roared to life. He waved my thanks aside and followed me all the way back into town. When I finally got my car to a mechanic, it took them a full ten minutes to find what he had taped.

TRAFFIC KINDNESS

I was driving home from work on a crowded city street—parked cars on either side, traffic going about twenty-five miles per hour. I noticed a group of prepubescent boys on bikes, bobbing and weaving through traffic, being quite reckless and taking silly chances. Suddenly I realized that one of the boys was holding on to the door handle of my car, pedaling like mad to keep up. I honked and pulled over, gesturing for him to talk to me. First he took off, but then he circled back, looking sheepish and expecting a lecture, no doubt. His friends gathered around to see what would happen.

I got out of my car slowly, thinking about what kind of life this child must have to be willing to take such chances and wondering what I could possibly say that could make a difference. The words just tumbled out of my mouth. "I don't know you," I said quietly, "but I want you to live to a ripe old age with all your arms and legs intact." The boy looked at me, smiled, said "Thanks," and rode off. I don't know if I made a difference, but I pray I did.

A LESSON ON THE ROAD

When I was sixteen and learning how to drive, I motioned to a driver to go ahead of me. He didn't acknowledge what I had done, and self-righteously I said, "Well I'll never do that again!" My father asked me to pull over and said, "You're not kind to people because they'll thank you. You're kind to people because it's the right thing to do. You're kind to people because it helps the other person and because it helps you." That was fifteen years ago, and I've tried to live my life from that perspective ever since. I can still hear my father's gentle voice asking me, "Your attitude, action, comment—will it add to the sadness and hurt of the world? Or will it add to the love and the kindness that might heal us and make us whole? It's your choice."

* * *

Too many people are ready to carry the stool when the piano needs to be moved.

—Anonymous

BEYOND WORDS

I was at the main train station in Tokyo, trying to take the bullet train to Kyoto. The station is huge; there are more than fifty departure and arrival platforms, and all the signs are in Japanese. No one I tried to get directions from spoke any English. The time I was supposed to depart was nearing, and I had not yet found the correct platform. In a state of near panic, I went to a ticket window and explained my predicament to the agent, only to be met with his blank stare. Obviously, he spoke no English.

Pointing to my tickets and to my suitcases, I communicated my desperation to him in body language. Suddenly, his face showed signs of comprehension. Jumping across the counter, he grabbed one of my suitcases with one hand and my arm with the other and began to run. For the next five minutes or so, the ticket agent and I were engaged in a weird dance as we weaved across platforms, bridges, and alleys, through tunnels, and past crowded passages, suitcases in hand, to the one platform he knew was the right one. Literally seconds after he pushed me and the suitcases into the car, the door closed and the train pulled out of the station.

THE RESCUE

I was heading with my girlfriend through the Santa Cruz Mountains on the way to a Samoyed breeder to pick up a new puppy. It was raining hard, and the dirt road that was supposed to lead directly to the breeder's farmhouse was now simply a wide rut. My Honda was having trouble with the mud and the steep incline, and there was an ugly drop into a now rushing creek bed to one side of the road. Suddenly we ground to a complete stop—stuck in heavy mud, with no tools, phones, or (so far as we knew) humans for miles.

We waited for about an hour, debating the merits of hiking in the pouring rain back toward civilization (miles away), trying to get the car unstuck (our attempts so far had just wedged us more firmly in the muck), and yelling (very, very loudly) for help. We were sitting in the car feeling hopeless when we saw faint lights behind us—we hadn't heard the engine because of the rain.

A young man in a VW stopped. He was headed toward his home beyond the breeder's farm. He told us he had towing equipment and would come back and help us and would also let the breeder know we were still on the way. We settled back to wait, half doubting he would return. In forty-five minutes he was back with a truck and towing equipment. Half an hour later, we sat in a warm kitchen out of the rain, with hot cups of tea, surrounded by tea-cup-sized Samoyeds.

WHEN
YOU LEAST
EXPECT IT

SURPRISING ACTS
OF KINDNESS

Our brightest blazes of gladness are commonly kindled by unexpected sparks.

—Dr. Johnson

ONE OF THE BEST CHRISTMASES

Driving home from a last-minute Christmas shopping trip, my father was carefully navigating his way through the heavy falling snow. About a half-mile from our farm-house—the only one for miles—we spotted a car in the ditch and stopped to investigate. It was empty. The blowing snow all but obscured the lane up to our house, but I could see that the lights were on and we never left the lights on.

As we stumbled in our front door, we were greeted by the refugees from the abandoned car, a stranded family of four. They began apologizing for being in our house, but Mom just said, "Shush, you did what you had to do," as she began preparing hot drinks and food for us all.

It seemed so natural to expect them to stay the night, so my brother and I eagerly began getting acquainted with our new friends. Farm life was lonely for the two of us, age eight and ten, and the company of other boys was always welcome. That night the full force of the storm hit and by morning it was obvious that our guests would not be able to continue their journey to Minnesota for Christmas. There was two feet of snow everywhere and probably no snowplow for days. To four small boys it was paradise.

Mom just took us aside and we began to rewrap and address presents for our newly-found extended family. Unbeknownst to us, the father had gone back to their car to collect their Minnesota presents and was doing the same. It was one of the best Christmases I can remember.

THE WINTER COAT

A friend of mine was going back east to college. Not only was it going to be her first time away from home, but, even more overwhelming to a California baby, she was going to experience her first true winter. She spent months looking for the perfect winter coat, a task all the more difficult when even long pants seemed stifling. Finally, two days before her departure, she found a coat that would keep her from getting frostbite and maybe even homesick. Unfortunately, the store didn't have the size she needed; but another location thirty miles away did. In desperation, she told the saleswoman her situation, and the saleswoman consoled her, promising that she would "take care of it." Two days and a few logistical phone calls later, the saleswoman met my friend at the airport gate, perfect-fitting coat in hand. The saleswoman was definitely acting above and beyond the call of duty, since I'm sure her job description didn't require her to deal with airport parking.

THE CASE OF THE BIZARRE POST

The year I went away to college was a very difficult transition for me. I lived in Oregon and had hauled my earthly possessions all the way to Southern California to a place I had never been before and was surrounded by people I didn't know. As is probably true with many people, I got quite homesick and many times contemplated going home.

Although the highlight of the day for many students is getting letters from home, my mailbox was frequently empty, which did nothing to ease my unhappiness. One day when I went to the mailbox, there was a postcard staring out at me. I sat down to read it, expecting a note from someone back home. But I became increasingly confused as I read the postcard and understood none of it. It was a full news report about a woman named Mabel and the recent birth of her very ugly baby. I double-checked the address and, yes, it was addressed to me—with no return address. Still confused, I took the card back to my dorm room and forgot about it.

Several days later I received another postcard, this one delivering news about Maybelline, Mabel's copycat cousin who had also had a baby, and their matching FBI husbands. Soon after another card arrived, then another. Each card grew progressively more bizarre, full of news of people riding horses into Safeway, remembrances of Mabel's birthday on a yacht in Madrid, and so on. I began to really look forward to the next installment, interested to see what this mystery writer would come up with next. I was never disappointed.

Eventually, the cards stopped coming, right about the time I had begun to feel a part of college life. They had been such an entertaining distraction that I hardly noticed the change at first.

When I went home on a break I visited an old high school friend and told her about my mystery correspondent. She hesitated a moment, then told me that her mother had wanted to make sure I got some mail while I was at school but didn't have a lot to say, so she just made up things.

I have saved all her postcards and still bring them out to read now and then whenever I need a lift.

••

When a blind man carries a lame man, both go forward.

—Swedish proverb

HAPPY NEXT BIRTHDAY

My ten-year-old granddaughter Anika is a big baseball fan. I have cable television, and we have spent many a wonderful time together rooting hard for a Cubs victory. She also plays on a local girls softball team and practices her batting in my backyard. My dog is the "catcher" and dutifully returns any errant pitches to the pitcher.

A couple of years ago we were shopping the baseball card collection at an antique show, and Anika really wanted this Ryne Sandberg card—he is our favorite player and Anika even had a number 23 stitched onto her sweatshirt. After some discussion, however, we decided that five dollars was just more than we could afford, so we handed the card back and continued to discuss the other cards. Out of nowhere a hand reached in with the card and a five-dollar bill, and the man turned to my granddaughter and said, "Happy next birthday!" He turned and was gone before we could even thank him.

* *

To receive everything, one must open one's hands and give.

—Taisen Deshimaru

Corporate Kindness

I am a corporate lawyer, and several years ago I was at my first closing. The investment banker came to deliver a check for $55 million to my client, and before my client arrived, I went to the Xerox machine to copy the check for our records. I put the check in the feeder of the copier, and it promptly shredded it! I told the banker about the mutilated check, and a moment later my client arrived, eager to receive the money. The banker looked at me and said to the client, "I can't believe it! I forgot the check!" He left and returned an hour later with a new check, and I kept my job.

....

All things whatsoever ye would that men should do to you, do ye even so to them: for this is the law of the Prophets.

—Matthew 7:12

*Injustice, poverty, slavery,
ignorance— these may be
cured by reform or revolution.
But [people] do not live only
by fighting evils. They live by
positive goals, individual
and collective, a vast variety
of them, seldom predictable.*

—Sir Isaiah Berlin

He that is kind is free, though he is a slave; he that is evil is a slave, though he be a king.

—St. Augustine

In the long run, we will get no more than we have been willing to risk.

—Sheldon Kopp

A Boy by the Side of the Road

When I was in my third year of high school, I was driving through a very rich neighborhood late at night when I spotted a small boy walking along the road. He seemed so out of place that I pulled over to see if he needed any help. When I opened my door I could see that he was about eight years old and was crying. I asked him where he was going and if he needed a ride home, but he wouldn't answer me. Finally I just said, "Here, get in the car and we'll go get some ice cream or something." He willingly got in but then wouldn't answer anything with more than a yes or no.

Before starting the car, I got a twenty-dollar bill out of my purse and told him to hold it until we found an ice cream store. As we were searching, I kept asking where he lived and offering to take him home. Finally he said, "No, please, they're mean to me. I ran away."

I asked him if he lived with both his parents, and he told me that he lived with his father and stepmother. He said he wanted to be with his mother, but she lived in Texas.

We drove around for about an hour, never finding an open ice cream store, and he still refused to be taken home. Finally he told me where his best friend lived, so I took him there and gave him my phone number. On the way back to the car I remembered the twenty-dollar bill I had given him and assumed he still had it. When I got in the car the money was lying on the passenger seat. I remember smiling, hoping he would be okay and thinking that he had probably just had a fight with his father.

A week later I got a call from his friend's parents, telling me that they had found iron burns across his back and other cuts and bruises. He ended up being sent to his mother in Texas after a big court battle. It made me feel so blessed to have been able to play a part in helping him escape from the brutal world he had been living in.

THE LAMP AND THE BUS DRIVER

My sister lives in a small town in Germany. She wanted to have a nightstand lamp repaired, so she wrapped it up and put it in a shopping bag and boarded the bus to the nearest large town. When she arrived at the repair shop, she realized she had left her bag on the bus. She called the bus company and asked if they would return the shopping bag to her the next day if it were found.

The next morning she went down to the bus station at the appointed time and they handed her the bag with the lamp in it, only now the lamp worked perfectly! She called the bus company and discovered that the bus driver—a man obviously very handy with such things—had discovered the bag, seen that the lamp was broken, and between routes had repaired it. The next day the bus driver was delivered a still-steaming loaf of my sister's fantastic homemade bread.

....

Caring is a reflex. Someone slips, your arm goes out. A car is in the ditch, you join the others and push. . . . You live, you help.

—Ram Dass

THE VIEW FROM THE ESCALATOR

When I was working in Washington, D.C., I used to take the Metro to work. Every morning as I got off the subway and rode the escalator up to street level I would hear the same man's voice booming in the manner of Robin Williams in the movie *Good Morning Vietnam*, only his message was, "Good morning, America!" I was not amused. I was always in a hurry, he was half blocking the exit off the escalator, and sometimes he would look at me and speak directly to me. I for one just wished he would go away.

Then one morning as I stepped onto the escalator (it was Christmas season), I could hear this beautiful, lyrical, a cappella version of "Joy to the World" greeting me. The familiar song was being sung in a clear tenor, and the words and music were so bright and beautiful that I felt like I was hearing the carol for the first time. My heart skipped a beat and tears came to my eyes as I rode up the escalator bathed in the blessing of this perfect song.

Sure enough, it was Mr. Good Morning America, standing off to the side, today with his eyes closed, giving us all a wonderful Christmas present as we stepped onto the pavement to face our workday. I have carried that stranger's precious gift with me ever since and I often silently thank him for giving me a memory I will always cherish.

CITY KINDNESS

I was about to go into the hospital for breast cancer surgery when there was a knock on my door. It was a man from the utility company telling me that the next week they were going to tear up the street in front of my house to put in a new sewer. My face fell and I said, "This is terrible! I'll just be back from the hospital convalescing from cancer surgery." The man turned and left. I later found out that they totally rearranged their schedule so that the work on my street wouldn't begin till several weeks later to give me some peace and quiet when I first got home! For years later, I would see that guy working on the sewers around town and we'd wave to one another.

....

For beautiful eyes, look for the good in others; for beautiful lips, speak only words of kindness; and for poise, walk with the knowledge that you are never alone.

—Audrey Hepburn

A New Television

Two years ago, a sixty-eight-year-old woman was the victim of a burglary. She lived simply on a fixed income, and the only item of value—her television—was stolen. After saving for nearly a year, she bought a new one. Then, returning home one afternoon from a visit with her sister, she found a police officer waiting for her. Her home had been burglarized again, and again her television had been taken. This news left her scared, shaken, and without access to what was a regular part of her day.

This time the story turned out differently. After hearing her plight, the officer in charge of the investigation took up a collection at the police station and negotiated a deal with a local electronics store that resulted in a brand-new television arriving in time for her sixty-ninth birthday.

Agape is understanding, creative, redemptive goodwill toward all men. Agape is an overflowing love, which seeks nothing in return. Theologians would say that it is the love of God operating in the human heart. When you rise to love on this level, you love all men not because you like them, not because their ways appeal to you, but you love them because God loves them.

—Martin Luther King, Jr.

Where People Gather, Kindness Is Never Far Away

W hen most people think of the telephone company, kindness is not a word that comes to mind. But telephone companies are staffed by people, and where people gather, kindness is never too far away. A service representative for a Midwestern phone company had taken a call from an elderly woman wanting to make payment arrangements. She learned during the course of the call that the woman was housebound due to bad weather, was out of heart medication, and, because of her tight budget, was eating only one meal a day.

Many phone calls later to different volunteer agencies in the area, the operator had arranged for the woman to receive medication and a weekly visit by a nurse, regular deliveries of food, and assistance with utility bills. All of this was accomplished without fanfare and without ever telling the woman who had done the legwork.

THE FORGIVEN DEBT

I had a client who owed me a good deal of money. Eventually she stopped seeing me, but each month I would send her a bill and receive no response. Finally I wrote to her and said, "I don't know what difficulty has befallen you that you are unable to pay me, but whatever it is, I'm writing to tell you your debt is forgiven in full. My only request is that at some point in your life, when your circumstances have changed, you will pass this favor on to someone else."

Oh I am a cat that likes to
Gallop about doing good.

—Stevie Smith

THE MOMENT THAT UPROOTED
MY PREJUDICE

I am an immigrant from the old Soviet Union. I brought with me many dreams and misconceptions, and, I am sad to admit, some prejudices. One day after I had been here for only a very short while I had spent what seemed at the time to be a very large sum of money on a Fast Pass bus ticket to make sure I could always get to school and around town. I had just bought it, and when I returned home it was gone. I don't know how or where I had lost it, and even though I had put my name and address on it I knew that anyone else could use it very easily. I had to face the fact that it was gone. I felt very depressed.

Then the doorbell rang. Standing there was a black woman with my Fast Pass in her hand. She told me she had found it on the sidewalk a few blocks away and handed it to me. At that moment everything changed. I will never again generalize about people because of their color, and I will never forget that woman.

An Unexpected Apology

I was driving home from work one day and the traffic was terrible. We were crawling along and out of nowhere this guy just pulls out onto the shoulder, passes a whole line of cars, and cuts me off so quickly I have to slam on the brakes to keep from crashing into him. I was really rattled.

About fifteen minutes later, I'm stopped at a light and I look over and there is the same guy next to me, waving for me to roll down my window. I could feel my adrenaline starting to flow and all my defenses coming up, but for some reason I roll down the window. "I am terribly sorry," he says. "Sometimes when I get into my car I become such a jerk. I know this must seem stupid, but I am glad I could find you to apologize." Suddenly my whole body relaxed and all the tension and frustration of the day, the traffic, life, just dissipated in this wonderfully warm, unexpected embrace.

···

Do not wait for leaders, do it alone, person to person.

—Mother Teresa

FORGIVENESS

Several months ago, I found myself driving in L.A. during rush hour. Traffic was heavy, but everyone was going quite fast. Suddenly a white Mazda in the slow lane spun out, doing four complete circles across the freeway. I stared in disbelief as cars swerved to avoid the whirling white dervish. By some miracle, all the traffic missed the car, which came to rest on the opposite side of the freeway, in the fast lane, facing the wrong way. Everyone just continued on as though nothing had happened.

I pulled off the freeway, got out of my car, walked to the Mazda, opened the door, and pulled out a sobbing, woman who kept saying, "Did you see what they did? They ran me off the road." I put my arms around her and finally she calmed down enough to explain that a blue Bronco had forced her off the road, causing her car to spin out. There we stood—two women, total strangers, comforting one another on a busy freeway, when a blue Bronco pulled over and stopped. A woman jumped out, also crying. She ran over to the woman in my arms, saying over and over again, "I am so sorry; I didn't see you; please forgive me." The first woman turned from me to the newcomer, and they melted into a sobbing embrace of "please forgive me's" and "it's okay's." When both women had calmed down, we figured out how to get the Mazda turned in the right direction, and, once that was accomplished, jumped back in our own cars and went on our way.

LATE TO SCHOOL

I was always a very conscientious student, and in my entire school career I was late to class only once. I was seven years old, and, of course, it had to happen when I was just starting a new school (my third that year). Even I though it wasn't my fault, I was terribly embarrassed and afraid, particularly since I was very shy and did not know the other children. Tears were streaming down my face as I ran the final blocks to school. As I passed the house across from the school, a well-dressed man came to the gate. I had never met him, but I knew his name because he was one of my town's most prominent citizens. He said to me, "Little girl, what is the trouble?" I blurted out my story, and he pulled out an immaculate white handkerchief, wiped away my tears, and told me that the dour Mrs. Morris—the school principal—was a friend of his and he would go with me to help sort out the difficulties.

He took my hand and walked me to school. In the principal's office he made excuses for me and asked that as a special favor I be let off without a reprimand. When he finished talking, I could see that "dour" Mrs. Morris was having trouble not laughing. I was never again afraid of her. She walked me to my class and told the teacher that new children were allowed one unrecorded tardy. I was an instant celebrity—a shy stranger no longer.

I Say a Silent Blessing Each Time I Drive By

I have always believed in guardian angels, but I had no idea mine would be in the form of a gynecologist! I was devastated to learn at age nineteen that I had an incurable and painful ovarian disease. Many difficult decisions followed, and my experience with the medical community left me despairing and disheartened. I searched for ten years to find a physician who was not only knowledgeable but compassionate, and I had nearly lost faith.

Then I noticed a story in the local paper about a new gynecologist who was establishing a practice in our small town. I hesitated, but finally decided to go. To my amazement he said if it would help, I could stop by often just to chat—free of charge! The only "help" I had ever received before was a new prescription for pain medication. Through his genuine concern this doctor managed to motivate a very depressed person in physical and emotional pain to return to life.

He kept careful track of my progress as I joined aerobics, lost weight, and became able to sleep through the night with less pain. When I needed a hysterectomy, he held my hand during the anesthesia, sent flowers to my hospital room, and even reduced my bill when he found out my insurance would not cover it all.

Two years later my life feels worth living, and I say a silent blessing of thanks each time I drive by his office.

THE SECRET GARDENER

I moved into a new house a few years back. It was the first time I'd had a yard of any size. There was a small lawn, about thirty rosebushes, six camellias, five rhododendrons, and numerous smaller plants, which, at the time, I could not even name. I was a bit overwhelmed and not doing a very good job of maintenance—especially cutting the grass.

After a few weeks, I noticed—vaguely—that something seemed different when I came home one evening. But I didn't pay too much attention. Then one day I came home to find freshly cut grass, precisely trimmed around the edges, all around the sidewalks and driveway. I realized that someone had been weeding and pruning almost every day while I was away at work. Finally I caught the culprit in the act—my eighty-six-year-old neighbor, Mr. Okumoto. It's now been seven years and he's still doing it, not only my yard, but the yard behind his house and the one on the other side of his. He's now ninety-three and I don't know how long I'll be blessed with his diligent work. Maybe forever.

Suspiciously Kind

I had just moved to the San Francisco Bay Area and was worried about what seemed to be the increasing frequency of carjackings. Whenever I drove I was constantly aware of my surroundings and was always taking steps to avoid becoming a statistic. One morning I was in a particularly bad area, sitting at an intersection waiting for the light to change. As I looked across the street, I saw several men grouped around a stopped car. One man was moving in and out of the driver's side with such intensity and effort that he looked as though he was using all his strength.

My heart jumped into my throat as I thought I was witnessing someone being carjacked. But before my brain could come up with any action to take, I realized that the man's car had stalled, and with the help of the other men he was trying to push it to the side of the street. As I watched, they pushed it to safety and after a wave and a nod they all walked off in different directions. Total strangers helping someone out. I felt like crying. Such unexpected sweetness. It's good to be reminded that as cruel and crazy as the world can seem sometimes, much of the time people really are kind.

NEVER JUDGE A MAN BY HIS HAIR

Many years ago my husband and I relocated to California. As we were preparing to move, I was warned many times to "watch out for those long-haired, drug-crazed hippies." Shortly after our arrival, our new neighbors took us to a hidden beach they had found near Half Moon Bay. It was a beautiful cove that was accessible only by going down a steep, sandy embankment. We had a wonderful day, and built a great driftwood campfire. As the temperatures began to drop and the fog started rolling in, we decided to head home. My husband and our neighbors packed up the coolers and blankets and began the strenuous trek up the embankment. I followed, carrying my baby daughter while my cranky two- and four-year-olds struggled through the shifting sand.

We were soon left behind and within moments ground to a discouraging halt—the four of us close to tears. Suddenly up at the top of the hill two such "long-haired hippies" appeared. My heart stopped. I felt completely defenseless and alone, stuck partway up a steep embankment with three small children. The young man quickly took off his backpack, scurried down the hill, and to my horror grabbed my oldest son, hoisted him onto his shoulders, and climbed back to the top, where he handed him to the young girl accompanying him. He returned twice to pick up my other two children and ferry them to solid ground before returning one more time. He looked me straight in the eye and said, "Are you alright?"

I realized that he was more than ready to pick me up and carry me to the top of the hill as well! I laughed and assured him that relieved of my burden I could make it myself. I thanked him, and as it turned out, they were searching for a place to camp that evening. I hope our well-built campfire warmed them as much as their sweet assistance warmed me.

A MONTH FULL OF FLOWERS

When I graduated from college I took a job at an insurance company in this huge downtown office building. On my first day, I was escorted to a tiny cubicle surrounded by what seemed like thousands of other tiny cubicles, and put to work doing some meaningless thing. It was so terribly depressing I almost broke down crying. At lunch, after literally punching out on a time clock, all I could think about was how much I wanted to quit but couldn't because I desperately needed the money.

When I got back to my cubicle after lunch there was a beautiful bouquet of flowers sitting on my desk. For the whole first month I worked there flowers just kept arriving on my desk. I found out later that it had been a kind of spontaneous office project. A woman in the cubicle next to me brought in the first flowers to try to cheer me up, and then other people just began replenishing my vase. I ended up working there for two years, and many of my best, longest-lasting friendships grew out of that experience.

It is godlike for mortal to assist mortal.

—Pliny the Elder

As a child I understood how to give; I have forgotten this grace since I became civilized.

—Ohiyesa

The Unexpected Compliment

A number of years back, my six-year-old son and I had gone shopping at one of those giant discount toy stores with toys piled to the ceiling. We had just come around the corner of an aisle when I saw a young, long-haired, bearded man in a wheelchair. He must have been in some terrible accident, because both his legs were missing and his face was badly scarred. Just then my six-year-old saw him too and said in a loud voice, "Look at that man, Momma!"

I did the normal mother thing and tried to shush my son, telling him it was not polite to point, but my son gave a hard tug, broke free from my hand, and went running down the aisle to the man in the wheelchair. He stood right in front of him and said in a loud voice, "What a cool dude earring, man! Where did you get such a neat earring?"

The young man broke into a grin that lit up his face. He was so taken aback by the compliment that he just glowed with happiness, and the two of them stood there talking awhile about his earring and other "cool stuff." It made a life-long impression on me. For I had seen only a horribly scarred man in a wheelchair, but my six-year-old saw a man with a cool dude earring.

PROFOUND CONNECTION

When I was in college I attended a lecture one evening on hypnosis by a blind hypnotist. At the end of the session we did a prolonged relaxation exercise, and I walked out of the room with a completely different body than I had walked in with. It was a very powerful experience of actually feeling myself as a body for the first time in my life. As I was walking across a bridge on the way home from the lecture, a man jumped out of the bushes and tried to hit me. It was really strange—here was a random act of physical violence coupled with an incredibly powerful experience of kindness that had moved me into my body. The violence is now just a memory, but the hypnotic journey into my body forever changed how I feel.

··

Let us not be satisfied with just giving money. Money is not enough, money can be got, but they need your hearts to love them. So, spread your love everywhere you go.

—Mother Teresa

A GIFT OF FEAR

Two days before my fiftieth birthday I had a heart attack. It was a most surprising random act of kindness. I had lived the previous thirty years of my life as a powerful, successful, and amazingly productive man. I had also lived so cut off from my emotions that I couldn't even fathom what the whole fuss about feelings was all about. I had worn out the efforts of three good women, took pride in my unfeeling logic, denied that there was anything wrong or missing in my life, and was prepared to march stubbornly forward.

Until I was felled and terrified by my own heart. That experience unlocked a lifetime of buried emotions. So, without knowing it, when the doctors revived me, they delivered me to a life fuller and more beautiful than I had ever imagined.

* * *

Fear grows out of the things we think; it lives in our minds. Compassion grows out of the things we are, and lives in our hearts.

—Barbara Garrison

WHO WAS THAT MASKED WOMAN?

I was at my sister's house, and I was there to rest. She lives in a big fancy house on the outskirts of Denver, and all around her house is a canal. It's very safe, so I thought I would go for a little run—that's putting it too strongly—a little amble along the canal. I put on my little ambling shoes and started walking. All of a sudden, two women came running up the canal, screaming, "He's back there! He's back there! He's back there!"

I have no idea why I did this, but I took one, two, three steps in the direction they were pointing, and here comes this stark naked man with an erection running toward me. Without thinking, I let loose my loudest ear-piercing yell, and he stops in mid-stride. I mean totally stops. Here I am, a woman standing there looking fiercely determined, and he stops, turns, and runs in the other direction. Then I went to the women who were still hysterical and helped them calm down. The man hadn't touched or hurt them. Finally I flagged down a trucker, and as the trucker called the police on his CB, I disappeared. I'm sure those two women were wondering, who was that masked woman?

THE EYE OPENER

I was living in Chicago and going through what was a particularly cold winter, both in my personal life and outside. One evening I was walking home from a bar where I had been drinking alone, feeling sorry for myself, when I saw a homeless man standing over an exhaust grate in front of a department store. He was wearing a filthy sport coat and approaching everyone who passed by for money.

I was too immersed in my own troubles to deal with him, so I crossed the street. As I went by, I looked over and saw a businessman come out of the store and pull a ski parka out of a bag and hand it to the homeless man. For a moment both the man and I were frozen in time as the businessman turned and walked away. Then the man looked across the street at me. He shook his head slowly and I knew he was crying. It was the last time I have ever been able to disappear into my own sorrow.

* *

Concern should drive us into action and not into depression.

—Karen Harney

Don't Give Up

I had been stuck for years in a place that refused to change. Everything seemed hard, solid, and unmovable. Making the most difficult and painful decision of my life, I left the woman I had shared my life with for fourteen years and started an avalanche of change that forced me down a dark and anguished path of sadness and growth. Every time I thought I had reached the bottom, another trapdoor would open below me. I had spent almost a year jettisoning useless baggage until I felt stripped raw, empty-handed and emotionally exhausted.

The one tangible thing I had done was to buy a new car—a nice one—a car that was soft and comfortable and responsive. I was sinking, but I was trying to find a way out. One night I woke up in a cold sweat from a devastating nightmare. In the dream everything had been taken from me. In the last scene I stood on a street corner watching my car being driven away, knowing that I had nothing left and no way to go on,

The next morning, as I dressed to go into San Francisco for a meeting, I was filled with a sense of foreboding. The dream clung to me and wouldn't let go. I arrived half an hour early and found a parking place right in front of the office I was visiting. It was a beautiful fall morning, and I decided to calm my nerves with a walk. I was carefully locking my briefcase in the trunk when I was approached by a

continued

very polite, elderly Chinese man who was completely lost. I spread his map over the trunk of my car, showed him where he was, and traced the best route to his destination for him on the map.

He thanked me profusely and headed off. That small exchange boosted my spirits considerably and helped to dissipate the cloud of impending doom. First a perfect parking place, then a simple but honest human interaction. I put a dime in the parking meter and, after registering my ten minutes, the dime fell out of the empty cash-box hole and back into my hand. Things were definitely looking up.

But when I returned from my walk twenty minutes later, my car was gone. I reached in my pocket but my keys were not there—I had left them dangling from the lock on the trunk. The day unfolded like a bad dream: I called the police and they came to the wrong address; when they finally arrived, I couldn't remember my license plate number (the plates had only been on the car for a week); I got a ride back home and spilled a full cup of coffee down my leg and into my shoe.

My ride dropped me off at the home of the woman I had left almost a year before. I had lent my old car to a close mutual friend who was staying with her, and I explained what had happened and said I needed my old car back. The woman I had loved for fourteen years looked at me and without a shred of compassion said, "Well, there's a message from the gods!" It pierced my heart like a knife. I knew she would regret having said it, but that no longer mattered.

That evening I stood outside on the deck of my house thinking about everything that was gone, everything that no longer mattered. I never imagined life could be this painful or this lonely. I realized my self-support system had been reduced to driving my car, playing golf, and reading. And now my car was gone, with my golf clubs and reading glasses safely locked in the trunk. I didn't know whether to laugh or cry so I did both. From behind me, inside the darkening house, I could hear music. Kate Bush was singing the haunting refrain to Peter Gabriel's cry of despair: "Don't give up . . . don't give up . . ." In front of me, the sky bled a breathtaking deep purple-red sunset. I stood there watching the sunset dissolve into a stunningly beautiful and clear night. I knew that for all I had lost, I had lost nothing.

That night I went to bed exhausted but at peace for the first time in many, many months. I was awakened at midnight by a night-shift dispatcher for the San Francisco Police Department. My car and everything in it had been recovered undamaged.

Blessings Multiplied

One Kind Act Leads to Another

With every deed you are sowing a seed, though the harvest you may not see.

—Ella Wheeler Wilcox

FEEDING A HUNGRY MAN

One day, as I was opening the door to the coffee shop across the street from my office, a panhandler stopped me and asked me to buy him a meal. He insisted on giving me a few bucks and explained that it wasn't quite enough for a burger, but he was really hungry and could I help. I took his money, fully intending to make up the difference. Apparently the proprietor saw everything, because when I got to the head of the line he said he'd be happy to give me a full meal for the few bucks I'd been handed. He said he couldn't risk becoming known for serving free or cheap meals to the homeless 'cause he'd have them lined up out the door, but he was happy to get food to the hungry through a third party like me. Clever workaround, I thought. And funny that it never happened again.

....

Good will is the best charity.

—Yiddish Proverb

As much as we need a prosperous economy, we also need a prosperity of kindness and decency.

—Caroline Kennedy

The government in which I believe is that which is based on mere moral sanction . . . the real law lives in the kindness of our hearts. If our hearts are empty, no law or political reform can fill them.

—Leo Tolstoy

COFFEE FOR EVERYONE

The main conceit of the 2000 Kevin Spacey film *Pay It Forward* is that if one person does a kindness for three strangers, and those three people each do kindnesses for three strangers, and so on, one person can change the world. Rarely do we see this acted out in the real world the way it was cinematically—one scene finds a man giving away his brand new Jaguar to a guy having car troubles—but on a smaller scale, these sorts of random niceties happen far more often than you might think. Today, it's selflessness at a small coffee house in Bluffton, South Carolina.

It all started two years ago at Corner Perk, a small, locally owned coffee shop, when a customer paid her bill and left $100 extra, saying she wanted to pay for everyone who ordered after her until the money ran out. The staff fulfilled her request, and the woman, who wishes to remain anonymous, has returned to leave other large donations every two to three months.

"People will come in and say, 'What do you mean? I don't understand. Are you trying to buy me a coffee today?'" the shop's owner, Josh Cooke, told the local news. "And I say, 'No, somebody came in thirty minutes ago and left money to pay for drinks until it runs out.'"

It took a while, but word has started to spread around the tiny coastal town, home to about 12,000 people. Now, more and more customers have been leaving money to pay for others' food and drink. Cooke says some people don't even buy anything when they come in; they just stop to donate and head right back out.

A medium cup of coffee at Corner Perk costs $1.95. That may not seem like a lot, but for a family struggling to save money in these tense and difficult economic times, two bucks saved at the right moment probably feels like a million. And a jolt of generosity is a better pick-me-up than caffeine any day of the week.

....

By the accident of fortune a man may rule the world for a time, but by virtue of love and kindness he may rule the world forever.

—Lao Tzu

THE GUARDIAN ANGEL

One Friday afternoon I was on my way to set up for a book fair in San Francisco. Waiting at a stoplight in front of the convention center, I noticed a handicapped woman on the street corner. She was sitting against a fence, a walker by her side, surrounded by what was probably all of her belongings. As I watched, another woman, perfectly coiffed, in high heels and a power suit, came up to her with a bag. Without a word, the businesswoman proceeded to lay out prepared food, which she had obviously bought "to go," around the street person so that she could easily reach the food from a sitting position. The homeless woman looked on in grateful amazement, as if her guardian angel had appeared out of nowhere just in time. In fact, she had. Three days later, when I was leaving the convention center, I passed the same woman leaning against the same fence. This time, a man in a van was at the stoplight, honking and holding money out to the woman. She was trying to move, but couldn't get up. Quickly, I ran to the van, grabbed the money, and brought it to her. I felt so happy to see people taking care of this woman, and pleased that my weekend was bracketed by tokens of generosity.

Believe nothing, O monks, merely because you have been told it. . . . Do not believe what your teacher tells you merely out of respect for the teacher. But whatsoever, after due examination and analysis, you find to be kind, conducive to the good, the benefit, the welfare of all beings—that doctrine believe and cling to, and take it as your guide.

—Buddha

THE CHIPPED, BLACK PIANO

When my daughter Anne was eight she decided she wanted to play the piano. I did not own a piano and had no intention of buying one; making my mortgage payment was challenge enough. I was teaching to make ends meet, and my daughter was spending time at an underfunded day care center after school. The place had limited play resources: a few rejected balls from the elementary school, a hand-me-down pool table complete with warped cue sticks from the 1970s, and an old wall piano from when public schools still had the funding for classroom music.

Anne and her best friend, the sheltered daughter of two Indian engineers, had become fast experts at the game of pool. When that diversion got old, Anne explored the piano. I would pick her up at five o'clock, and find her there, pitifully alone, plunking away. Rick, the retired teacher's aide who ran the place, begged me to give her lessons—probably to restore a semblance of harmony to the end of his day.

Meanwhile we had adopted the couple across the street as surrogate grandparents. My own family lived out of state and I was desperate for connections. Jerry was a retired screenwriter, and his wife Esther, a lovely woman with sparkling blue eyes and a tendency to make everyone feel like they have all the talent and beauty in the world, was a model. I'd taken to dropping by to talk to Jerry about my own burgeoning writing. He functioned more as a cheerleader than an actual mentor; he rarely read anything I wrote. What he did instead was listen to my tales of rejection letters and churning projects, and share his own antidotes.

Esther and Jerry had a piano—black, chipped around the edges, music piled haphazardly on its top along with yellowed newspapers and unpaid bills. I pictured Esther pounding out show tunes when they entertained back in the sixties.

It wasn't that often, but when I had to rush to the market or take a walk to clear my head, I'd send Anne across the street to their house where I knew she'd be supervised. When I returned, I'd hear her "practicing" her untutored piano pieces from the day care center.

Anne's birthday is two weeks after Christmas. I am always broke two weeks after Christmas. Her presents tend to be in the form of "I Owe Yous"—in the summer we'll go to Disneyland, that sort of thing. The year she turned nine I took her to Cocoa's for her birthday. It's not as pitiful as it sounds; my daughter was in love with the place. On your birthday the waiters and short order cook put a candle in a scoop of ice cream and sing.

When we got home, two delivery men were sitting on our porch. My first thought was that I'd been robbed; it was seven o'clock at night, late for a delivery. Besides, I hadn't ordered anything. The man in charge informed me they were there to make an easy delivery—Esther and Jerry's piano from across the street. It was their gift to her. Random and unexpected, it has made a huge difference in my daughter's life. She is headed off to college this year where she will study music.

In Praise of a Wonderful Nurse

A few years ago my three year-old son had a nasty fall and ended up at the local hospital. It turned out that the fall was the least of our worries. The doctors found a tumor the size of a softball in his left lung. We were all scared to death, and the doctors were none too optimistic. Throughout this traumatic development, a male nurse showed great compassion toward my son.

Surgery was ordered immediately for the next day, and my son had to go through a tough procedure to get him ready. To my distress, the wonderful nurse was just about to sign off for the day, and the nurse replacing him was one who hated her job. I casually mentioned to the man that I wished he was going to be on duty instead.

A little while later he reappeared and stayed with us, helping out even though he was off duty. He even arranged to change his shift the next day so that when my son came out of surgery he would be there to soothe his fears. I will never forget what he did, and today when I look at my son, who is better than anyone thought possible, I truly believe that the sincere caring of this nurse was instrumental in his being able to keep trying.

The world is in desperate need of human beings whose own level of growth is sufficient to enable them to learn to live and work with others cooperatively and lovingly, to care for others—not for what those others can do for you or for what they think of you, but rather in terms of what you can do for them.

—Elisabeth Kübler-Ross

THE MENDING DOG

I was living the artist's dream in a cottage in the Australian bush, when my American boyfriend flew me to visit him in Brisbane, where he was based. Upon arrival, I was greeted by an enormous, overweight dog. Cassie waddled over to check me out. It was love at first sight as the Rottweiler followed me from room to room.

Cassie was a leftover from my boyfriend's broken marriage. Not only that, she needed to be re-homed.

"She's adorable, but I can't have a dog. I travel a lot. And I can't even afford to feed myself," my boyfriend said. I protested weakly.

But Cassie was determined. Three days later, I was the proud owner of my first Rottweiler.

Then I took Cassie to the local vet for her first routine check up and received a shock—Cassie was full of heartworm, and the prognosis was bad. Yet losing her was out of the question.

In the process of the long and costly indoor cure, dog and owner bonded deeply. I was forced to learn everything I could about raising a dog, and in doing so, I discovered that I was a very capable person—far more so than I had believed myself to be. For the first time in my erratic artist existence, my life became organized, and even my art benefited from having a companion who patiently waited for me to finish work so we could go for a walk.

My love for Cassie knew no bounds. And as my love, devotion, and daily care for her grew, I felt myself blossom as a person. My life transformed from one of lonely struggle and self doubt to one of deep joy and confidence.

By adopting an overweight, unwanted dog, I had saved Cassie's life. And without a doubt, Cassie had saved mine.

....

Kindness is the better part of goodness.

—W. Somerset Maugham

THE OFFER OF AN OLD COAT

I had an old trench coat that was balled up on the floor of my garage gathering dust near the washing machine. It was raining. It was unusually cold (for California, anyway).

I was driving home when I saw a man in a short-sleeved shirt wandering through our neighborhood, pushing a shopping cart. He was dripping wet and walking painfully slowly.

I paused at the intersection to my street and watched him for several minutes, thinking. My heart was heavy seeing him move so slowly, so wet, so cold. I suddenly remembered the crumpled-up coat. But what if I needed it sometime in the future? Then a story I had once heard at a church conference came to mind:

Two boys walked down a road that led through a field. The younger of the two noticed a man toiling in the fields of his farm, his good clothes stacked neatly off to the side. The boy looked at his older friend and said, "Let's hide his shoes so when he comes from the field, he won't be able to find them. His expression will be priceless!" The boy laughed.

The older of the two boys thought for a moment and said, "The man looks poor. See his clothes? Let's hide a silver dollar in each shoe and then we'll hide in these bushes and see how he reacts to that, instead."

The younger companion agreed to the plan and they placed a silver dollar in each shoe and hid behind the bushes. It wasn't long before the farmer came in from the field, tired and worn. He reached down and pulled on a shoe, immediately feeling the money under his foot.

With the coin now between his fingers, he looked around to see who could have put it in his shoe. But no one was there. He held the dollar in his hand and stared at it in disbelief. Confused, he slid his other foot into his other shoe and felt the second coin. This time, the man was overwhelmed when he removed the second silver dollar from his shoe.

Thinking he was alone, the man dropped to his knees and offered a verbal prayer that the boys could easily hear from their hiding place. They heard the poor farmer cry tears of relief and gratitude. He spoke of his sick wife and his boys in need of food. He expressed gratitude for this unexpected bounty from unknown hands.

After a time, the boys came out from their hiding place and slowly started their long walk home. They felt good inside, warm, changed somehow knowing the good they had done for a poor farmer in dire straits. A smile crept across their souls.

Inspired by the story, I drove home, took my coat from the garage, and went looking for the old man in the rain.

continued

I spotted him quickly—he hadn't gone far. The rain had let up some, and I pulled up alongside him and asked him to come over.

He hesitated, then walked closer. I asked if he had a place to stay. He said he did and that it was close. I offered him my jacket. He looked stunned, like I was violating some accepted code of conduct. I urged him to take it. He slowly reached out and took my old coat. He smiled.

So did I.

We all have poor farmers toiling in the fields of their trials and difficulties along the roads of our lives. Their challenges might not be known to us. But their countenances often tell a story of pain. We have opportunities to hide shoes or hide silver dollars in them.

This day, this time, I removed a "silver dollar" from the floor of my garage and slipped it in an old man's shoe. My life was blessed for having done it. And I think the old man's life may have been blessed by it as well.

When I hear stories of kindness being done to others, I'm inspired to do the same. I think most of us are like that. We need each other's inspiration as we travel life's highways, trying to figure it all out.

AT AN INTERSECTION

A tired-looking man in well-worn clothes stood at the intersection wearing a large sign that read: HAVE FAMILY, WILL WORK FOR FOOD. I had passed him many times as I made my way around town, yet somehow I never got around to offering help to this fellow traveler as I went about my busy week.

One day, as I was going past the same intersection, I saw him once again steadfastly standing there. The traffic had stopped for a red light, and in the lane to my left a woman quickly got out of her car with two full bags of groceries, which she promptly handed to the man. They exchanged a few words before the light changed, and she jumped back in her car and drove away. The man's face lit up, his weariness lifted by this unknown woman's kindness. Carefully hugging the groceries, he slowly walked away from the crossroad. His radiant smile said it all.

In a fraction of a moment's time his life had been changed—and hers, and mine, and everyone else who sat in their cars and witnessed the exchange. The traffic still flowed, everything was the same, yet it was so very different.

Such an Expression of Decency

To many people civil servants and lawyers rank at the bottom of the list of those from whom you would expect unsolicited acts of kindness. Jerry Curtis knows better. Curtis, a fifty-year-old assistant attorney general with the Department of Justice, had been battling serious stomach problems and cancer of the lymph system. He was operated on and then began a lengthy regimen of chemotherapy. He tried to go back to work, but the treatment left him weak and vulnerable. Within a couple months all his sick leave had been depleted, and he was forced to get by on what savings he had.

One day Jerry found a check from his employer in his mailbox. It turned out that fellow Department of Justice employees from all over the state had donated four months of their collective sick leave and vacation pay to ensure that Jerry could focus on recovering his health without having to worry about how he was going to pay his bills.

"These people are so decent," said Jerry. "People I did not even know donated their time. It is just overwhelming; it's very difficult to describe how I feel. It's one of the strongest expressions of decency I've ever known people to make, and I don't even know who did it. I can't even give it back to them if I don't use it all. But if someone else needs it, you know I'm going to be the first one to donate it."

A DEBT REPAID

I was working one day when I heard a very distressed voice coming from a nearby office. A woman I did not know had been counting on borrowing money from a colleague but circumstances made it impossible for him to help her. I have no idea what possessed me, but without even asking what she needed it for I found myself going to the bank and withdrawing $1,000 to lend to a complete stranger.

Several months later, after a series of life's ever-surprising turns, I found myself jobless, homeless, and, I thought, friendless. I also needed medical care in order to even begin looking for a new job. The woman to whom I had lent the money was not in a position to return it, but she ended up repaying me anyway—and then some. First, she had the medical training necessary to help me get back on my feet; then she had her son, who owned a small moving business, come collect my belongings; and she arranged for her boyfriend to stay with her and let me stay in his apartment. I now had the three things a homeless person needs most: an address, a telephone, and a shower. As a bonus, her boyfriend had a lovely cat who gave me great comfort in that difficult time.

It wasn't too long before I found work and moved to a home of my own. That was thirteen years ago. The woman and I have stayed friends and even became business partners. To her it was a miracle that anyone could give so much money to a stranger; to me the miracle was that anyone could come up with such a basketful of solutions custom-made to fit my needs.

PAYING THE RENT

I recently went through a painful yet relieving divorce after seventeen years of marriage. I needed a place to live with my two boys, and my sister and brother-in-law graciously suggested we move in with them. It was a wonderful thing for them to have done, but I soon realized that we needed to find a home of our own. But how could I afford it? A single mother with two children—rent, daycare, groceries, clothes, health insurance, car payments, etc. It seemed overwhelming but I knew in my heart that somehow it would work out.

I found a small house and proceeded to move in, not knowing how I was going to make ends meet. Two weeks later a dear friend stopped by my work. He had heard about my divorce, and he and his wife wanted to help. He offered to pay the rent for me. I thought it was for one month, but every month I received a check from them for my rent.

It was such an unbelievably generous thing to do. He did not want me to repay him and asked only that if possible I return the favor to someone else in need someday. It turned out that when he was struggling in medical school someone had done this for him.

My religion is very simple. My religion is kindness.

The Dalai Lama

How Can We Leave a Man to Die?

How easy it is to come to political conclusions, and how difficult it is to carry out some of those decisions in the world! Like many other border states, California has gone through its share of political pronouncements over the economic burden of illegal immigrants. The solutions have often been harsh, and, for a thirty-eight-year-old man named Enrique, threatened a death sentence.

Enrique slipped across the Mexican border three years ago with a dream common in this country: to work hard and make a better life for himself. He worked the fields of California and lived in the shadows of society, until he showed up at a county hospital with a large tumor on the back of his head. Diagnosed with a treatable case of lymphoma, Enrique came up against a harsh reality: his cancer was completely curable, but without treatment he would be dead within six months, and the state's "safety net" for medical treatment no longer pays to care for illegal immigrants.

Indeed, the hospital routinely turns away those too poor to pay, but Enrique's life-and-death plight caused many of the health-care professionals involved to pause and reconsider. Meetings were held, ethics debated. As his treating physician said: "Ethically, the situation is not at all unclear—this is a matter of life or death. If Enrique were a wealthier person or born in a different place, he'd be getting treatment. The system has gotten so crazy that we can look at a young, healthy guy and say, 'Sorry.'"

But instead of saying sorry, a small group of health workers decided to do something about it. Doctors at the hospital donated their time to treat him, but the treatment itself—radiation, expensive drugs, and hospital stays—also cost a lot. So they approached a number of pharmaceutical companies and two offered to donate medication. Then they went public and donations began flowing in for the rest of the expenses.

Now Enrique will get his chance at life because enough people cared.

....

Happiness is a by-product of an effort to make someone else happy.

—Gretta Brooker Palmer

MORE THAN ENOUGH

A friend who was working in the Dominican Republic with Habitat for Humanity had befriended a small boy named Etin. He noticed that when Etin wore a shirt at all it was always the same dirty, tattered one. A box of used clothes had been left at the camp, and my friend found two shirts in it that were in reasonably good shape and about Etin's size, so he gave them to the grateful boy. A few days later he saw another boy wearing one of the shirts. When he next met up with Etin he explained that the shirts were meant for him. Etin just looked at him and said, "But you gave me two!"

....

Engrave this upon my heart: There isn't anyone you couldn't love once you've heard their story.

—Mary Lou Kownacki, OSB

THE 360-DEGREE TURNAROUND

I had just moved out of a recovery house after spending six months battling an addiction to alcohol and drugs. I was standing at a bus stop looking through the classifieds, hoping to find a job I was capable of doing. Without a high school education and with my work experience limited to waitressing, the options seemed depressingly limited. At that point my self-esteem was stuck to the bottom of my shoes, and it diminished with each ad I read.

I looked up from the paper to see an elderly man sitting in his car. He asked me if I wanted a ride and I accepted—knowing what a foolish thing I was doing and even secretly hoping that he would put an end to it all for me. He asked me where I was going and what I was doing. I said I did not know. Then he simply asked me, "If you could do anything you wanted to do, what would it be?"

I blurted out that I would go back to school. I immediately felt stupid for saying it because I doubted I ever could. A few minutes later he pulled into the parking lot of the local community college, pointed out the admissions office, and told me I would find what I needed in there. Trembling and insecure, I filled out the registration papers.

As I write this, I have received my associate of arts degree and am planning to study toward a bachelor's in journalism and a master's in psychology. My life has turned around 360 degrees, and I owe a lot of that to a man whose name I don't even know.

A WISH FOR KINDNESS

Just before Christmas I was on the F train going uptown. At West 4th Street a young man boarded with a boom box. He explained, loudly and enthusiastically, "I'm trying to stay out of trouble tonight, so I'm offering you a dance."

Only a few of us looked up. Then he plugged his iPhone into his boom box and proceeded to dance his heart out. This included back flips, trapeze moves with the handrails, and body spins on the ground with just one hand. By this time all eyes were glued on him. A young boy next to me yelled out in sheer delight, "Wow—that's amazing!" We all shared his sentiment, and many passengers gave generously when he walked by with his donation container afterwards.

Then, at the other end of the car, a homeless man boarded with a plea for help. He was disheveled and without any dance routine or music act to offer. All he had was a wish for kindness and an outstretched hat—one that remained empty among this group of recent donors.

That is, until the dancer went right up to the homeless man just before the doors were to open at the next stop and spilled out all of his earnings into his outstretched hat and said, "Merry Christmas, man."

TWENTY CRUMPLED DOLLAR BILLS

My wife teaches piano lessons to kids and adults. One day a young man called to ask about lessons. He explained that he was living in his car but really missed playing the piano; it was something he'd done until mental illness took hold and his life unraveled. He couldn't afford her usual fee, he said, but he promised to pay her twenty dollars from the money he panhandled on the street. She readily agreed.

Every week he showed up right on time, usually with twenty crumpled one dollar bills in his pocket, which he'd count out one by one. In the spring he'd sometimes bring her berries he'd picked in a local park. He played very well and rarely missed a lesson. And my wife would always give him a sandwich and a piece of fruit when he left.

Then one day he stopped showing up. Didn't call. Nothing. Just vanished.

That was about ten years ago. Last year he called one day out of the blue to say he'd moved across the country, remarried, and had a new baby. He was working and saving some money for a piano.

More Than I Ever Needed

During the Depression my grandmother was a society matron in Cleveland, and, as she put it, "quite taken with" herself. One morning she found a basket of food on her doorstep. It made her furious that anyone could think that she was some poor needy person. Not knowing what to do, she put the basket in the kitchen without even bothering to unpack it. The next morning another basket of food was on her front step. By the end of the week she had five food baskets beginning to clutter the kitchen, and she decided that the least she could do was to pass the food along to those who were really needy. The baskets continued for a couple more weeks, and my grandmother realized that she had begun to look forward to finding someone who needed them. When the morning deliveries finally stopped, she starting making her own food baskets to give away.

The moral of the story? Said my grandmother, "Someone knew I really was a poor needy person and found the best way possible to help me."

....

When you are kind to someone in trouble, you hope they'll remember and be kind to someone else. And it'll become like a wildfire.

—Whoopi Goldberg

A POWERFUL NOTE

One night I was working late at the office on a deadline. I went out for a quick bowl of soup, which I ate sitting at the bar. There was only one other person there—a thin, middle-aged man with longish gray hair who seemed very sad. Politely, but with an edge of desperation, he was trying to get a conversation going with the bartender. She wasn't all that busy, but she seemed preoccupied and answered his questions very curtly.

I was torn between the desire to offer some comfort and the knowledge that I would already be up half the night meeting my deadline. Next to my bowl of soup I left a five-dollar tip and a note saying, "Be nice to that man. He is very lonely."

I thought no more about it. A few months later I went to the home of a seamstress who had been recommended to me. When she opened the door I saw that it was the bartender. She recognized me immediately, smiled, and invited me in. There on the living room couch sat the man who had been at the bar. They both laughed at my surprise. She pointed to the mantelpiece and there, resting in a place of honor, was the note I had written to her.

KINDNESS
AFTER LOSS

GRACE FROM FAMILY
AND FRIENDS

What do we live for, if it is not to make life less difficult for each other?

—George Eliot

HEALING TEA

My husband and beloved friend died very suddenly last October. Knowing how difficult the first Christmas without him would be, I decided to take my adult daughters to New Orleans for the holidays, hoping that different surroundings would make it a little easier. I was mistaken—nothing could ease the pain.

We decided to make the eight-hour drive home on a cold and dreary Christmas Day. You would think that the radio would be filled with Christmas songs, but instead every song sang out words of love and loss. The clouds and grayness of dusk mirrored my grief, and after a while I couldn't stand the confinement of the car any longer and asked my daughter to pull over and let me out.

I walked in the damp weeds beside the highway, sobbing in pain while my daughters followed slowly on the shoulder of the road. Suddenly, out of the enclosing darkness came the voice of a woman asking me if I was all right. She came to me and held me in her arms, and, with my daughters following, took me in her car to her home and then served us tea. Before seeing us on our way with renewed spirits, she led us to a nearby town famous for its beautiful Christmas lights. She was truly a Christmas angel.

An Anonymous Gift

The fall semester of my senior year in college was a particularly stressful one. My mother had just died after a battle with cancer, and I knew it would be difficult to cope with this loss and also juggle a campus job and a full course load. I never imagined I would be as unhappy as I was by the end of the semester. One day, after spending many hours studying for finals, I checked my mailbox and found two tickets for a John Cougar Mellencamp concert the next evening. There was a note attached that said, "Relax and enjoy yourself!" No name, no return address.

I was thrilled to be able to go to the concert but felt even better just knowing that someone had noticed how difficult the changes in my life had been. I asked all my friends, and everyone denied having given me the tickets. I have no idea who was so kind, but whoever it was helped me to remember that people do care.

••

What one does is what counts and not what one had the intention of doing.

—Pablo Picasso

THE TRUE MEANING OF FRIENDSHIP

When I was eight years old my family moved. I was the new kid coming into a new school, and I was pretty nervous, but the transition turned out to be a wonderful one. On my first day my teacher turned me over to a classmate named Beth with instructions to introduce me around. Beth made me feel so welcome, and she and I quickly became best friends. She got me to try out for cheerleading with her and taught me how to do back handsprings. For a few years we were inseparable. Then one day we had a fight—the kind that seems so big and important to kids—and although we remained friends, the special bond was broken and we gradually drifted apart.

During sophomore year of high school, Beth was killed in a car accident. Even though she and I moved in different circles by that point, I was overwhelmed by the hurt. And not being one of Beth's current friends, I was outside the circle of close friends mourning her death. This made things even more difficult, because I was left alone with my grief.

I graduated from high school last year, and Beth's mother came to see me. She brought me fifty dollars from Beth's life savings as a graduation gift. She told me she wanted to give a little something of Beth to her closest friends. Then she had a party for all of Beth's old friends to give us a chance to get back together and remember why we were friends in the first place.

Beth's mother's act of kindness changed me forever. Not only did she give me a part of Beth, but she gave me the comfort, acceptance, and understanding that I had not received two years earlier when Beth died. She taught me that you can never take love and friendship for granted and that they will always live in the hearts of those who experience their true meaning.

···

T'was her thinking of others that made you think of her.

—Elizabeth Browning

I feel no need for any other faith than my faith in the kindness of human beings . . . I am so absorbed in the wonder of earth and the life upon it that I cannot think of heaven and angels.

—Pearl S. Buck

THE GRACE OF A GOOD FRIEND

The approach of my daughter's high school graduation had been emotionally unsettling; I was so proud and happy for her, and yet I was already dreading her eventually leaving the nest. On the morning of her graduation I received a telephone call informing me of the death of one of my oldest and dearest friends. She'd had lung cancer. I was devastated by the news and thrown into a state of emotional overload. I felt like I could neither properly grieve my friend's death nor celebrate my daughter's graduation.

At the ceremony, with "Pomp and Circumstances" playing in the background, another dear friend appeared, carrying an armload of long-stemmed yellow roses. She plucked one out and handed it to me with a hug and a kiss and moved on to find other mothers with graduating children.

I watched her go, overflowing with the love she had imparted, and remembered that only a few years earlier she had lost her husband, the love of her life for more than twenty years, to the same deadly disease that had taken my friend that day.

THE HOUSE FIRE

We recently had the traumatic experience of having our house burn down, followed by the equally unsettling experience of trying to deal with the insurance company. How do you prove what you lost when it is completely and totally gone?

Our home was built over fifty years ago and, surprisingly, the city still had original blueprints on file. This proved at first to be more of a problem than a help, because we had completely remodeled the house five years before it burned, adding on an entirely new floor, extending the house out in the backyard, and building a real garage to replace the tiny box common to homes built in the thirties. The insurance company generously offered to replace the house as specified on the original blueprints. There had been a drawer full of pictures showing the remodeling job, but after the fire we had no proof of what we had lost. That drawer was gone along with everything else, and all we had was our word and the support of friends and neighbors.

Our story was covered in the local newspaper, and a few days later we received a photo album in the mail filled with pictures of our house! A man who had been an architecture student at the time we were remodeling our home had done a project on upgrading instead of destroying housing stock, and, unbeknownst to us, he had used our house as an example. He had done a complete photo history: before, during, and after. In his letter, he told us that it had all been quite a coincidence—the very day he started looking for a project was the first day our contractor showed up to start working. He had approach ed him to find out what they were going to do, and our contractor had been very cooperative, showing him all the plans and promising to show him details as he progressed. When we showed our insurance adjuster the photos, we could see him gulp—and they ended up paying even more than we had expected.

....

People say that what we're all seeking is a meaning for life. . . . I think that what we're really seeking is an experience of being alive, so that our life experiences on the purely physical plane will have resonance within our innermost being and reality, so that we can actually feel the rapture of being alive.

—Joseph Campbell

Compassionate the mountains rise,

Dim with the wistful dimness of old eyes.

That, having looked on life time out of mind,

Know that the simple gift of being kind

Is greater than all wisdom of the wise.

—DuBose Heyward

Practice Random Acts of Kindness!

❖ Go to your child's class and talk about random acts of kindness. Then have the kids put together a booklet of the random acts of kindness they have done for others and things others have done for them. Ask them to go home and teach their parents the idea and come back to school the next day with stories from their families.

❖ Spend half an hour in a hospital emergency room and do one random act of kindness that presents itself.

❖ Offer to help people who could use assistance to cross streets—seniors, the blind, small children.

❖ Plant a tree in your neighborhood.

❖ The next time someone speaks to you, listen deeply without expecting anything.

❖ Find someone you're close to and sit back to back with him or her. For a few minutes disclose the random acts of kindness they have done for you while they just listen. Then switch and listen to the wonderful things you have done for them.

❖ Yes, it's a drag, but why not put your shopping cart back in its appointed place in the parking lot?

❖ Write a note to the boss of someone who has helped you, thanking him or her for having such a great employee.

THE CHOICE

I have a friend, Franziska, who lives in a small village in Austria. She will be eighty next March. During the war, her husband, a simple, uneducated, Catholic farmer, decided he couldn't serve in Hitler's army because it would be an immoral act. My friend supported his decision even though they were desperately in love and she knew that his resistance would mean risking his life.

Eventually, her husband was convicted of treason and condemned to death. The day before his execution, Franziska went to visit him one last time in Brandenburg Prison near Berlin. After watching him being cruelly hurled off a truck, hands and feet bound, she was led by two guards into a room with a long table and two chairs. As she and her husband began to sit across from each other, one of the guards moved the chairs so that when they were sitting, they would be barely able to reach their hands across the table and touch. After an unimaginable last conversation, it was time to part. The other guard offered to bring the prisoner out, and the heartless guard left. The second guard then turned away from the couple long enough for them to rush into a last embrace. Waiting until their sobs quieted somewhat, he then said quietly, "It's time to go." A token act of kindness for a Nazi soldier, perhaps, but that man gave them one more moment to experience an extraordinary love.

THREE STRIKES

California recently enacted what is euphemistically called the "three strikes and you're out" law. It decrees that anyone convicted of a third felony is to be sentenced to a minimum prison term of twenty-five years to life. The campaign for this law had been characterized by the all-too-present fear of and anger about violent crime; but the law itself went much further, sentencing any third-time felon to a lifetime in prison regardless of the nature of the crime. One of the first cases to be prosecuted under the new law, however, quickly ran into an unanticipated problem—the victim.

The criminal, a forty-five-year-old repeat petty offender, was spotted breaking into a car and trying to walk away with an armful of clothes. The police did their job, and the local district attorney geared up to enforce the new law, until the victim—a seventy-year-old woman—refused to cooperate because she was appalled at its harshness: "I just think it's really gross; I couldn't enjoy another sunny day myself if he was never going to see one." Instead of life in prison, the burglar was sentenced to four years—plenty of time to contemplate the compassion of his victim.

If I can stop one heart from breaking,
I shall not live in vain:
If I can ease one life the aching,
Or cool one pain,
Or help one fainting robin
Unto his nest again,
I shall not live in vain.

—Emily Dickinson

JELL-O

We had a wonderful, funny, caring neighbor named Ed whom we lived next to for fifteen years. Ed developed terminal cancer, and as he gradually weakened, his wife became the sole breadwinner. Knowing how difficult just the daily routine was, I began cooking dinner for them one night a week. Ed and I shared a love for Jell-O, and each week I would try out a new variation. Since my family did not really care for Jell-O, this was a special treat for me as well.

Every Wednesday night at six o'clock I'd bring over their dinner, and every Wednesday at seven o'clock I'd receive a call from Ed, thanking me. Sadly, this ritual lasted only a few months; Ed passed away on Thanksgiving.

I had put that time out of my mind until about a year later, when I was making Jell-O and all those times with Ed came flooding back. Shortly before he died, Ed had written me a beautiful note thanking me for what I had been doing. As I was mixing the Jell-O I wished I had thanked him for the weekly gift he gave me. Through those times with Ed I learned that it truly was better to give than to receive, and you cannot give kindness without spreading some of it on yourself.

My Brave and Compassionate Nephew

One Saturday evening I received a long-distance phone call and learned that a very close, dear friend had died tragically. The unexpected news was quite a blow. I was in terrible pain and tried calling my three sisters, hoping to find one of them at home. On my first two calls I got no answer. On my last call, my sister's son answered and, still trembling, I explained my reason for calling. He said he would try to find his mother for me. The next thing I knew there was a knock at my door—it was my nephew. All I remember for the rest of that night was sitting on the couch in his arms, crying for what seemed like an eternity while he quietly held me and comforted me. I think often of what a brave and compassionate young man he was that night—he gave me much more than he will ever know.

....

The quality of mercy is not strained, —
It dropeth as the gentle rain from heaven
Upon the place beneath : it is twice blessed, —
It blesseth him that gives, and him that takes.

—William Shakespeare

THE OLD DOG

I used to jog through the park every morning, and I always went by an old woman who sat on a bench with a small, very old, mangy dog. One day I noticed her dog wasn't with her. For some reason I stopped and asked her where he was. Suddenly, tears started running down the lines in her face and she told me he had died the night before. I sat and talked with her for over an hour. Every day after that we would greet each other as I came by; sometimes I would stop and talk with her for a while. She was very lonely but also very strong, and to this day I think of her when I'm sad, and it makes me smile.

I firmly believe that mankind is so instinctively, unconsciously involved with the survival and growth of the species that when an individual attempts to live selfishly, he will either fail or fall into despair.

—Joyce Carol Oates

Practice Random Acts of Kindness!

- Buy a roll of brightly colored stickers and stick them on kids' shirts as you walk down the street.

- Make a list of things to do to bring more kindness into the world—and have a friend make a list, too. Exchange lists and do one item per day for a month.

- Spend a week just being aware of things in nature that befriend you.

- Open the phone book and select a name at random. Send that person a greeting card.

- Hold a random acts of kindness party where everyone tells the stories of kindnesses in their life.

- When someone is trying to merge into your lane in traffic, let him in—and why not smile and wave while doing it?

- All of you reading these words have loved someone, have done someone a kindness, have healed a wound, have taken on a challenge, have created something beautiful, and have enjoyed breathing the air of existence. Never doubt how precious, how vitally important you are. Every moment you make a difference. So, today, appreciate yourself as a random act of kindness.

Amazing Grace

We had just searched a small village that had been suspected of harboring Viet Cong. We really tore the place up—it wasn't hard to do—but had found nothing. Just up the trail from the village we were ambushed. I got hit and don't remember anything more until I woke up with a very old Vietnamese woman leaning over me. Before I passed out again I remembered seeing her in the village we had just destroyed and I knew I was going to die. When I woke again, the hole in my left side had been cleaned and bandaged, and the woman was leaning over me again offering me a cup of warm tea. As I was drinking the tea and wondering why I was still alive, a helicopter landed nearby to take me back. The woman quietly got up and disappeared down the trail.

....

Kindness is the language which the deaf can hear and the blind can see.

—Mark Twain

A Battered Old Teapot

My marriage had come apart in a dramatic and violent fashion that left me shaking and scared to death. I escaped with two small children, a broken-down car, and $423 in cash. I was so scared that I drove aimlessly for hundreds of miles, determined to get so completely lost that I could not be found. Not a single person knew where we had gone. After sleeping in the car for a couple of days, I found a run-down old house outside a small town and put down almost the last of my money for rent. I was scared and broke, but at least we had a place to start over. I spent the next day looking for work and came "home" to our sad and empty nest on the verge of tears, not at all sure we would make it.

There, sitting on the sagging front porch, were five bags of groceries; a large box of pots, pans, and kitchen utensils; and a vase of the most beautiful irises I had ever seen. I must have cried for ten minutes before I could pull myself together to unpack our miraculous gifts. No note, no explanation. I could not imagine who could have done it, who possibly could have known how desperate we were. That was many years ago, and sitting on top of my stove in my beautiful modem kitchen is an old, battered whistle-blowing teapot, reminding me when I boil water for my morning coffee of the beautiful gift of kindness that was given to me in my hour of greatest need.

Just Held My Hand

I am from a family of staunch Catholics, so my divorce was viewed as a disgrace and a scandal. My mother and I were estranged for over a year because of it. We started our reconciliation with tentative phone calls, letters, and my promise to come home for Christmas. Then she died unexpectedly on the first day of December. The plane tickets I had planned to use for a holiday reunion were instead used for her funeral. The black sheep returned to the fold.

For reasons of my own, I did not want to view the body in the casket. Many family members and friends questioned that decision, but I sat resolutely in the reception parlor as the others went inside for prayers. In the middle of the throng, my most "perfect and pious" aunt—the mother of the priest—quietly announced, "I think I'll stay here, too." She sat silently beside me and held my hand for the entire evening. The act was simple, the meaning immense. It happened thirteen years ago and I still cry when I remember how touched I was by her kindness.

....

When you cease to make a contribution you begin to die.

—Eleanor Roosevelt

TALKING ABOUT THE DEAD

M y son Tom was killed in the Vietnam War. When we received the news, my wife and our two other children who were still living at home had a very difficult time dealing with it. During the time we waited for his body to be returned home, made arrangements for the burial, and transitioned back into a semblance of normal life, I was the pillar of strength and stability. I thought I was just doing what I had been trained to do—stay strong and calm—but in reality I was scared to death to show any emotion at all out of fear that I would collapse into an emotional morass from which I could never recover.

As time went by I grew increasingly depressed and distant, even from my own family. I hardly knew what was happening. Life seemed very gray and joyless. Then one day about four months after the funeral, I received a call from a young man named Brad who had been a very close friend of my son. He asked if he could come over and I of course agreed, not really understanding what he wanted to talk about. When he arrived we spoke awhile about things Tom had liked to do and he told me some special memories from his relationship with Tom. Then he walked over, hugged me, and with tears streaming down his face said, "I just miss him so much."

Something inside me gave way and I broke down sobbing in this young man's arms. I cried and cried uncontrollably until it felt like my insides would spill out all over the floor. The two of us spent most of the afternoon in my study crying, talking, laughing, being embarrassed, crying some more, being embarrassed by being embarrassed, and finally, in a beautiful, drained, and painful state, just remembering how much we loved Tom and how much it hurt to have him gone.

....

Most people really believe that the Christian commandments (e.g., to love one's neighbor as oneself) are intentionally a little too severe—like putting the clock ahead half an hour to make sure of not being late in the morning.

—Søren Kierkegaard

Connections Through Cancer

My wife was dying of cancer, and during that time there were lots of nonrandom kindnesses in our lives. People who knew us did many ordinary and extraordinary things. But what touched many of us in our community happened early in my wife's struggle. We decided to have a water filtration system installed in our house to take the impurities out of the water. The plumber we contacted installed the system and wouldn't accept any payment. We found out later his father had died of cancer.

....

What good will it do you to think, "Oh, I have done evil, I have made many mistakes"? It requires no ghost to tell us that. Bring in the light, and the evil goes out in a moment.

—Swami Vivekananda

GIFT TO A STRANGER

One night, I was on the porch smoking a cigarette, while my lover was inside our house dying. We lived on a dead-end street in a residential neighborhood that had very little foot traffic, but that night a woman walked by. I looked at her; she looked at me. After she had almost passed the house, she stopped, turned back, and walked up to the porch. She told me that she had taken the bus from Fresno to find a job, that she had left her children with someone, and if she did not get back that night she would lose her kids. I called Greyhound and found out that the last bus to Fresno had left. We went around about what she would do. In the end I gave her $60 and she walked away. I did not then, nor do I now, believe her story. But I felt it was somehow important that I was being asked to give a gift to a stranger when someone I loved was about to die.

....

A kind heart is a fountain of gladness, making everything in its vicinity freshen into smiles.

—Washington Irving

Going On Without My Daughter

It was what will probably be the worst day of my life. A policeman had just come to our house to tell my husband and me that our nineteen-year-old daughter Amanda had been killed in an automobile accident. I remember immediately wondering if I could go on but soon decided that I had to find a path to survive a life without Amanda. Shock and numbness set in, and we started to do what one needs to do, calling the coroner, finding a funeral home and cemetery, notifying people of the death. The news spread quickly and our phone rang ceaselessly with friends inquiring what they could do for us.

One phone call came from a stranger, Susan. I recognized her name immediately as the mother of Amanda's classmate who had died the year before. Upon hearing her strong yet concerned voice a kernel of hope was born in me that I would somehow find a way to exist without my child. Susan and I made arrangements to meet the next week, and when I saw this vibrant woman who was still somehow able to live an active life amidst her grief, I began to trust that I too would find a path. Susan generously made herself available to me. We went for walks, had dinner, and chatted on the phone. I always came away with renewed purpose and endurance. We remain friends, almost twenty years later.

I now do my best to return to the world Susan's act of kindness, volunteering as a grief counselor for people who have lost children.

GETTING OUR FRIEND TO THE FUNERAL

I drive a taxicab in San Diego and have seen thousands of acts of kindness. One of the most wonderful came when the stepfather of our dispatcher died, and the dispatcher could not afford to fly back to New Jersey for the funeral. All day long pledges of money kept coming in over the radio. It was just like a private telethon. Cab drivers and even passengers who heard what was happening over the radio started emptying their pockets. We raised the plane fare in no time.

....

Kindness is the noblest weapon to conquer with.

—American proverb

There is a Law that man should love his neighbor as himself. In a few hundred years it should be as natural to mankind as breathing or the upright gait; but if he does not learn it he must perish.

—Alfred Adler

THE BOY SCOUT

When I was about twelve I used to visit this elderly gentleman who was a volunteer merit-badge counselor for the Boy Scouts. He would give us assignments until he thought we were proficient in a given subject. I did not know him long, but I admired him for giving so much to the community, even when he was in poor health.

One day I was scheduled to meet with him, but I forgot about it until some three hours later. I hopped on my bike and pedaled furiously to his home, all the while fretting about how poorly he must think of me for being an irresponsible Boy Scout. His wife answered the door and I blurted out my apology, but I could tell that something was wrong. She paused and then told me her husband had just died. Then she apologized for not having had time to inform our scoutmaster. I left her home wondering if somehow my failure to keep the appointment had disappointed him so much that he died.

Some thirty years later I told this story to a friend. I said that though I had long since realized that my lateness had nothing to do with his death, I could not help but wonder if I could have made a difference had I shown up on time. My friend quickly commented that my not being there was probably meant to be, since the situation would have been too traumatic for me. Hearing her say that was like a huge wave hitting me and lifting this heavy weight I'd been carrying for years. Now whenever I think of that kind old gentleman, I think too of the kind words of my friend.

A Good Heart

For several years I suffered with a failing heart. Last summer, as its strength waned dangerously toward complete failure, I was finally put on a list of patients waiting for heart transplants. By then my health was so precarious I was unable to do even the simplest act of shopping or cooking. The daily walk to the mailbox left me winded and weak. If I were to list all the acts of kindness that were shown to me during that time it would fill a full page of a newspaper. But one act stands out—that of the parents who lost their teenager in a horrible accident. In the midst of their anguish and indescribable grief, they gave me the gift of life: their child's heart. From the very depths of that heart—my heart—flow gratitude, sympathy, and prayers.

....

At some point your heart will tell itself what to do.

—Achaan Chah

The end result of wisdom is . . . good deeds.

—Babylonian Talmud

It's no use trying to be clever—
we are all clever here;
just try to be kind—a little kind.

—Dr. F. J. Foakes-Jackson

If you bring forth what is inside of you, what you
bring forth will save you. If you don't bring forth
what is inside of you, what you don't bring forth will
destroy you.

—The Gospel of Thomas

In Need of Neighbors

Twelve years ago I came home from grocery shopping to a message that my husband had been killed in a freak auto accident. Totally aside from the devastating emotional toll it took on me, I was completely unprepared to cope with the myriad things that needed to be done. Without asking, seemingly without any planning whatsoever, my neighbors simply extended their circle of chores to encompass my small farm.

One day my cornfield was harvested; repairs to my roof and barn just appeared. My vegetable garden seemed always weeded and more productive than ever before—soon vegetables that I didn't remember having planted were ripening. I would come home to find a pile of wood, cut and stacked and ready to get me through the winter. Pies, breads, jams, and cases of canned tomatoes appeared at my door and in my pantry.

It all seems so unreal now: whatever was needed simply manifested. When it was no longer needed, it no longer appeared. It was like some kind of beautiful self-correcting dance of kindness. I will be forever grateful to all those wonderful people.

Kindness is an inner desire that makes us want to do good things even if we do not get anything in return.

It is the joy of our life to do them.

When we do good things from this inner desire, there is kindness in everything we think, say, want, and do.

—Emanuel Swedenborg

Living the truth in your heart without compromise brings kindness into the world. Attempts at kindness that compromise your heart cause only sadness.

—Anonymous 18th-century monk

Practice Random Acts of Kindness!

- ❖ Write a letter of appreciation to that which in nature has been a safe place for you.

- ❖ As you go about your day, why not pick up the trash you find on the sidewalk?

- ❖ Write a card thanking a service person for his or her care and leave it with your tip. Be sure to include a very specific acknowledgment: "I appreciate the careful way you cleaned the room without disturbing my things"; "Your smile as you served me dinner really made my day."

- ❖ If you are in any of the helping professions, ask your clients to tell you their stories of random acts of kindness.

- ❖ For one week, act on every single thought of generosity that arises spontaneously in your heart and notice what happens as a consequence.

- ❖ A traveling salesman we know always carries cracked corn in his car and scatters it for birds during the snowy winter months.

- ❖ On Thanksgiving, call up everyone you know and ask them what they are thankful for so they can feel their own gratitude.

- ❖ Talk to people at work about one of your random acts of kindness and ask what one of theirs is. Disclosure stimulates us to do more by emphasizing the pleasure of giving with no strings attached.

I remember your saying that you had notions of a good Genius presiding over you. I have of late had the same thought—for things which [I] do half at random are afterwards confirmed by my judgment in a dozen features of propriety.

—John Keats

The center of human nature is rooted in ten thousand ordinary acts of kindness that define our days.

—Stephen Jay Gould

Service is the rent we pay for being. It is the very purpose of life and not something you do in your spare time.

—Marian Wright Edelman

The words of kindness are more healing to a drooping heart than balm or honey.

—Sarah Fielding

THE RESCUED WINDOW

During the first week of September 2011, our entire village was catastrophically flooded. Our home had nearly four feet of water on the first floor. During the initial weeks of gutting the walls and floors and removing everything ruined by water and contaminated mud every street had piles of filthy trash many feet high. The trash trucks were running constantly, but the piles would just rise back up. After many days of this, my husband and I were so exhausted and overwhelmed that we began just throwing things on the pile if they required too much cleaning.

A month or so later we had dinner with neighbors. After the meal they handed us a large package wrapped in brown paper. Inside we found a leaded glass window someone had made for my husband many years earlier. He had come across it in the debris and just couldn't face the task of cleaning the mud out of the intricate glasswork. Our neighbor explained that a co-worker had found the piece of glass on a trash pile while walking around taking in the devastation. He had taken it home, cleaned it completely, and wrapped it up to return to its owner. He told our neighbor he just knew we hadn't meant to throw it out. His random act of kindness lifted our very weary spirits during a very difficult time.

Live as if everything you do will eventually be known.

—Hugh Prather

A person who seeks help for a friend while needy himself will be answered first.

—The Talmud

Practice Random Acts of Kindness!

- ❖ Take the opportunity to tell friends about kindnesses you have experienced and ask about their experiences. Just talking about acts of kindness brings them alive in the world.

- ❖ Get your children to go through their toys and put aside those they want to donate to children who are less fortunate.

- ❖ Buy a giant box of candy at the theatre. Take one, and pass it down the row to share.

- ❖ Next time you go to the ice cream parlor, pay for a few free cones to be given to the next kids to come in.

- ❖ If you have an infirmed person living near you, offer to do the grocery shopping for him or her.

- ❖ Pick up the mail for a senior or someone else who could use the assistance.

- ❖ Send an email to someone you don't know and start a random acts of kindness email chain.

- ❖ If there is a garden you pass frequently and enjoy, stop by one day and leave a note letting the occupants know how much pleasure their garden gives you.

- ❖ Make a dedication on your local radio station to all those people who smiled at strangers today.

Sharing the Wealth

A Bounty for One and All

I am done with great things and big plans, great institutions and big success. I am for those tiny, invisible loving human forces that work from individual to individual, creeping through the crannies of the world like so many rootlets, or like the capillary oozing of water, which, if given time, will rend the hardest monuments of pride.

—William James

ED'S SHIP

Last year I had occasion to get acquainted with a homeless man who lived at the top of a freeway off-ramp in Los Angeles. Every day on my way to work as I sat waiting for the light to change I would talk to Ed about life, homelessness, hopefulness, and the weather—the weather being of vital importance to Ed. We became close, always asking about each other's family—mine in L.A., his on the East Coast. He rarely asked me for money, and I usually tried to bring him some food. Once when he had dental problems I brought him bananas, dried soup, and aspirin.

Ed had many other "regulars" who tried to help out. When I decided to leave L.A. for a job in Florida, I had one final detail to attend to—my car. It was an ugly 1972 Dodge Dart, but it ran great. I had put a lot of money into it, but the most I could get out of it was ninety dollars from a wrecking yard. I wanted it to go to someone who could and would make use of it, and Ed was the logical choice. He had dreams and plans; he wanted to return to trade school—he had had to drop out earlier when his books were stolen, then the bus schedules changed and they no longer went by the trade school.

The week before I left I made Ed the offer of the car or the money from the junkyard, whichever he wanted. With enthusiasm he accepted the car, going on and on about it being his house and the answer to his problems. We took care of the paperwork, I paid for his license renewal, and then I delivered the car with cans of oil, air and oil filters, and a trunk (he calls it his garage) full of paper plates, paper towels, canned food, clothes and—an L.A. essential—an earthquake kit.

As we stood next to the car on a Saturday morning, Ed said he had worked out a deal with a local parking lot owner: he would sweep the lot every day in exchange for a covered place to park his "house." He also told me that he had just been offered a job as a dishwasher in a new upscale restaurant near his off-ramp. It turns out that another driver who regularly gave Ed money and food had bought the restaurant and asked him to work there at a really good wage. As we hugged good-bye, I said, "Ed, it looks like your ship has come in." He replied with tears in his eyes, "Hell, it's not only come in, I get to go on board."

It is our special duty, that if anyone needs our help, we should give him such help to the utmost of our power.

—Cicero

Independence? That's middle-class blasphemy. We are all dependent on one another, every soul of us on earth.

—George Bernard Shaw

GIVING FROM WHAT YOU'VE BEEN GIVEN

All of my adult life has been spent working with the very poor and being filled over and over by those whom I have chosen to serve. I often do outreach among the homeless living in our local transit hub, trying to get as many as possible into shelters. Many of these people are afraid to go to shelters for fear of losing their few belongings, but they do not hesitate to sleep in the station because they look out for each other. When someone new arrives, the "regulars" are always available to assist him or her. Underwear and socks are like solid gold to the homeless, yet I cannot begin to tell you how many times I have seen someone give their spare pair to someone who had none.

I have never ceased being awed by their great ability to serve. One day during the evening rush hour a woman who was dressed in a very business-like manner, obviously rushing home from work, tripped and fell in a public area. Other well-dressed people continued on their way, even though it meant passing by her fallen body. But all the homeless folks in the area rushed to her assistance, helped her up, offered to make a phone call and get her medical assistance if she needed it. I could fill volumes with the stories I have been privileged to encounter. They give from their nothingness and with great freedom.

Sunshine on a Rainy Day

I have been going to the same bagel/coffee shop every Sunday for years. One morning, in the middle of a great dreary, drizzly weekend, I trudged in dripping wet with my newspaper carefully tucked under my overcoat and ordered my usual bagel with lox and cream cheese and an espresso. I was casually informed that my coffee had already been paid for. I looked around expecting to see some friend sitting somewhere but didn't, and when I asked, the young woman at the register just smiled and said, "Someone paid for twenty coffees, and you are number eight." I sat there for almost an hour, reading my paper, and watching more surprised people come in to find their morning coffee prepaid. There we all were, furtively at first and then with big funny smiles on our faces, looking at everyone else in the restaurant trying to figure out who had done this incredible thing, but mostly just enjoying the experience as a group. It was a beautiful blast of sunshine on an otherwise overcast winter day.

What you deny to others will be denied to you, for the plain reason that you are always legislating for yourself; all your words and actions define the world you want to live in.

—Thaddeus Colas

. . . .

A human being is a part of the whole that we call the universe, a part limited in time and space. He experiences himself, his thoughts and feelings, as something separated from the rest—a kind of optical illusion of his consciousness. This illusion is a prison for us, restricting us to our personal desires and to affection for only the few people nearest us. Our task must be to free ourselves from this prison by widening our circle of compassion to embrace all living beings and all of nature.

—Albert Einstein

DUSTY, THE HORSE

My husband and I travel a lot, and at the time this story happened I had a horse, a wonderful horse. We were out of town when a one-hundred-mile endurance horse race (that's a race where people from all over New England get together and travel as fast as they can for one hundred miles) went right past our driveway. My horse, whose name was Dusty, decided that she wanted to join the race. So she jumped over the fence. Galloped off. No saddle. Nobody on her back.

The next day when my husband and I came home there was a note on the front door from the sheriff saying that my horse had gone back to the barn on the other side of town where she had been born eighteen years before. So we drove there. It was a lovely old farm, owned now by people I didn't know.

The new owners were a man, his wife, and their children, two little girls ages seven and five. And sure enough, there in the corral behind the barn were the two girls and Dusty. The man told me that when they had gotten up that morning, the little girls had started screaming because at the top of the hill, with the sun rising behind her, was this beautiful palomino horse. They lured her into the corral and proceeded to spend the day brushing her and treating her a lot better than she had been treated for many years under my sometimes care.

They looked so happy. The seven-year-old girl turned to me and, with a trembling lip, said, "Can I ride her before you take her back?" I said that she could have her for another half-hour or so. And then I went to the local general store and bought a bottle of apple cider. When I returned, they told me they had always wished for a horse but their parents really didn't have the money for one. I sat them down and told them I was going to give them Dusty. And that I wanted them to promise me that someday when they were grown up they each would find a little girl—a little girl they didn't know—and give her some very special gift that she had always wanted.

Then we celebrated with a bubbling glass of apple cider, toasting to Dusty.

....

A person's true wealth is the good he or she does in the world.

—Mohammed

RETURNING THE KINDNESS

Folk wisdom tells us that "It is better to give than to receive." What it doesn't say is that it is also easier to give than to receive, at least for many of us. When we are giving, we are in control. We get to be the hero, the generous one, the kind one, the one to whom others are grateful. It is actually harder to be the recipient, for in the receiving role, we are not in control, we are in the passive role of being receptive, and we often feel beholden to the person who is giving to us.

I learned this first-hand with my cousin Marilyn, who is also a dear friend. She lives just around the corner, and she is always doing kind things for me: she picks up a case of cat food when she goes to Costco; she buys candles on sale and brings me some; best of all, she loves to cook (I don't) and she often invites me over for dinner. Sometimes I feel that our relationship is a little unbalanced, as if I'm her poor country cousin and she takes pity on me and feeds me. Of course, that's not true—it just feels that way occasionally.

She's also been there for me when big things happen. The day I took a nose-dive down a flight of stairs, dislocating my shoulder and fracturing my arm, she gave up her Sunday afternoon to follow the ambulance to the hospital and kept me distracted from the pain while we waited for the ER team to decide how they were going to treat my injuries. She then drove me home, stopping at the pharmacy to get the painkillers, fed me some soup and crackers, and tucked me into bed. Marilyn is like the big sister I never had.

Her boyfriend, John, has also been a kind friend to me. A retired cardiologist, he often answers my medical questions when I'm curious about something or other. He even made a house call to me in the middle of the night when I was so ill with who-knows-what and thought I was having a heart attack. He showed up at my front door with stethoscope, thermometer, and blood pressure monitor in hand—an angel of mercy indeed!

Finally, one day, I had the opportunity to return their kind favors. Marilyn and John were flying in his ultralight plane and crashed into an avocado grove. Both were seriously injured, spending a few days in the hospital before they were brought home to recuperate. I made pharmacy runs for them, picking up their prescriptions; I went to Chinatown to pick up soft noodles, some yummy soup, and other things I thought they could eat; I made trips to the grocery store every couple of days to get whatever they felt like eating. And while I wasn't happy that Marilyn and John were injured, I was happy to have the opportunity to take care of them, after the many times they had taken care of me. I could drive them where they needed to go, call and see what they needed from the store, pick up the mail, haul out the trashcans on pick-up day, and other simple things like that.

That old folk saying is right—it is better to give than to receive. But it's even better when you have the opportunity to do both!

I am of the opinion that my life belongs to the community, and as long as I live, it is my privilege to do for it whatever I can. I want to be thoroughly used up when I die, for the harder I work, the more I live. Life is no "brief candle" to me. It is a sort of splendid torch which I have got hold of for a moment, and I want to make it burn as brightly as possible before handing it on to future generations.

—George Bernard Shaw

PASS IT ON

In the mid-1980s, my husband and I were financially well off, so we decided to take our Christmas money and do something to benefit someone in need. We knew a couple struggling with a failing business, three young children, and the possible loss of their home. We gave them money and told them that we did not want to be repaid but that when they got back on their feet, they could pass it on to someone else in need. Just a few weeks later I met the recipient of our gift. She told me that part of our wish had already come true: they knew another family in even worse circumstances than they were in and had given half of our gift to them. What kindness! Our giving was from our surplus but their giving was from need.

. . . .

Whatever we do for someone else we do because it fulfills a need we have.

—M. Scott Peck

THE TURNAROUND

I had just completed my training as a chiropractor and I wanted to open an office. Then the perfect place just fell into my lap, but I didn't have any money. None. And I needed not only rent money, but money for a table, chairs, and so forth. I called a few friends but was only able to raise around a thousand dollars total—not nearly enough. Then I got a call from a man who was the cook at the school where I had trained. He told me to stop by because he had something for me. When I went over, he led me into the back room of the kitchen. There on a table was a large stack of money. Handing me a piece of paper and a pen, he told me to count the money and write up an IOU. It was around $6,000—an unbelievably trusting and generous gift.

After getting my office set up and beginning my practice, things suddenly started going very badly. Within a few months, nine friends and relatives died. Here I was trying to build a practice at the same time that I was being overwhelmed by grief and working under the added pressure that it was someone else's money I was working with. As a result the practice was not going well and I was rapidly approaching bankruptcy.

One day I woke up, went into the office, and decided that something good had to happen. So I gave my secretary a raise. She said, "You can't afford to do that," but I told her I couldn't afford not to. That day everything began to turn around, and I was eventually able to pay back the cook.

Random Act of Bridge Toll

My husband and I have a tradition that the first time we are crossing a toll bridge into a new city, we pay the toll for the random stranger behind us. We did this when we moved to San Francisco, and we still do it whenever we are vacationing and the opportunity arises.

....

Shall we make a new rule of life from tonight: always try to be a little kinder than is necessary?

–J. M. Barrie, *The Little White Bird*

Spare Change

Every day I walk down to the mall to get a cappuccino, and every day I get hit up for spare change. Every day. The panhandlers all have these wonderful stories, but you never know what to believe. After a while it gets to be an irritation, and then I find myself getting upset that I'm so irritated over what is really just spare change. One day this person came up to me and said, "I just ran out of gas. My car is about six blocks away from here, I have two kids in the car, and I'm just trying to get back home."

I said to myself, "Here we go again," but for some reason I gave him $10. Then I went on and got my cappuccino. As I was walking back to my office, I again saw the man standing by his car, which had run out of gas right in front of my office. Seeing me, he came over and said, "Thank you, but I don't need the full ten," and handed me $2.

Now I find that being asked for money no longer bothers me, and I give whatever I can every time I get the chance.

●●

He does well who serves the common good rather than his own will.

—Thomas à Kempis

Music for Struggling Families

An underemployed friend of mine was looking for a recording of a specific piece of classical music to use in a music appreciation class he teaches at a local senior center. He came across a recording of the piece by a young string quartet he'd never heard of. Curious, he Googled them and discovered that they were a struggling young group of immigrant Russian women, all highly trained but still waiting to get their big break. Moved by their story and their beautiful music making, he sent them a very small cash gift. Less than twenty dollars. It was all he could afford. He suggested that perhaps they could use the money to offer a free ticket to one of their concerts to someone without a job. They were so touched by his gesture that they decided to make two of their upcoming concerts free to anyone who was currently unemployed. And their families, too. The local papers picked up the story, and ticket sales for the rest of their season went through the roof. And several unemployed folks got to hear some gorgeous music, too.

BATHING THE FEET OF THE HOMELESS

I heard a kindness story on the radio the other day that just made me weep. Two retired men in the Sacramento area, a realtor and a beautician, started volunteering once a month to care for the feet of the homeless. One of the men bathes and gives foot massages and the other gives a pedicure. Neither of these men had ever volunteered their time to anything like this before. What really moved me was when they said it gave them far more than it took to show up once a month for a few hours. It gave them satisfaction beyond measure.

FOUR PRECIOUS PENNIES

It was Easter time and I was in People's Drug Store. I was maybe ten years old. There was a small Whitman's candy with a pixie doll on it for one dollar, and I wanted to get it for my mother. She was a widow with an eighth grade education raising six kids, and English was her second language.

I waited in line, and when it was my turn I handed the dollar to the clerk and she told me it was $1.04. I said, no, the sign said a dollar. She said there was tax. I was crushed. I said I really wanted to get this for my mother, but the clerk said there was nothing she could do.

I could feel my face getting red and my eyes started to burn with tears when I heard four pennies hit the counter and a woman said, "here honey, you take that to your mother." I was elated.

Some forty years later, I have been paying that gift back, and trust me when I tell you the rewards have never stopped flowing my way.

● ●

We must enhance the light, not fight the darkness.

—Aaron David Gordon

THE MAGIC DRAGON

Several years ago, when I was living in Chicago, I read in the newspaper about a little boy who had leukemia. Every time he was feeling discouraged or particularly sick, a package would arrive for him containing some little toy or book to cheer him up with a note saying the present was from the Magic Dragon. No one knew who it was. Eventually the boy died, and his parents thought the Magic Dragon finally would come forth and reveal him or herself. But that never happened. After hearing the story, I resolved to become a Magic Dragon whenever I could and have had many occasions.

* *

We do not remember days, we remember moments.

—Cesare Pavese

If you help others, you will be helped, perhaps tomorrow, perhaps in one hundred years, but you will be helped. Nature must pay off the debt. . . . It is a mathematical law and all life is mathematics.

—G. I. Gurdjieff

Kindness makes the difference between passion and caring. Kindness is tenderness, kindness is love, perhaps greater than love . . . kindness is goodwill, kindness says, "I want you to be happy." Kindness comes very close to the benevolence of God.

—Randolph Ray

For us, there is only the trying. The rest is not our business.

—T. S. Eliot

Waste no more time talking about great souls and how they should be. Become one yourself!

—Marcus Aurelius

Helping a Friend in Need

There was a time in my life when everything was working so smoothly, I found myself sitting at home one Saturday with all my work done, all my household chores completed: dishes washed, laundry folded and put away, house dusted, grocery shopping completed, and that delicious feeling of having nothing to do. Then I thought about a friend from work who was a single mother of two small children and never seemed to have the time for anything. I jumped into my car, drove over to her house, walked in, and said, "Put me to work." At first she didn't really believe it, but we ended up having a great time, cleaning like mad, taking time out to feed and play with the kids, and then diving back into the chores.

....

A soul occupied with great ideas best performs small duties.

—Harriet Martineau

RIPPLES

It was my fortieth birthday, and I'd celebrated it in Laguna Beach at an Indian Puja, where I'd spent the day in deep meditation. Driving back to L.A., I thanked God for the experience, as well as for the shortcut a friend had suggested. I guess the traffic gods didn't know that it was my birthday, because I hit bumper-to-bumper traffic anyway. Then I noticed a tollbooth up ahead. Unfamiliar with tollbooths in southern California, I grabbed a dollar out of my wallet. But as I neared, I was shocked to see the fare was $3.75! At that moment, my inner angel chimed in. "Great time to play 'anonymous angel.' You could pay for the car behind you, too!" I get it, I thought, feeling ripped off is the perfect time to practice generosity and get back in the universal flow of abundance. I looked in the rear-view mirror and saw . . . a Rolls-Royce!

"The car behind me is a Rolls!" I quipped to my inner angel.

"You have no idea the ripples this could cause," it continued. "This could inspire him to give his employees a raise, which enables a child to go to college, which leads to world peace."

I paid for the next two cars . . . and proceeded down the highway. Shortly thereafter, I noticed the Rolls on my tail. Fighting to protect my anonymity, I sped up . . . so did the Rolls. We raced down the highway. I began to laugh at the absurdity. After all, was it really worth getting a speeding ticket to remain anonymous? I allowed the Rolls to pass, and savored the sweet, yet perplexed look on the driver's face as he nodded at me in my old Honda. I thought about those ripples, and the vision of hope it gave me was the best birthday present ever.

. . . .

We make a living by what we get, but we make a life by what we give.

—Norman MacEwan

Kindness is the golden chain
By which society is bound together.

—Goethe

Whoever performs only his duty is not doing his duty.

—Bahya ibn Pakuda

GOLF IN THE INNER CITY

My brother is a teacher who doubles as the golf coach for an inner-city high school. On the first day, he had four excited boys—only one who had even played miniature golf—and no equipment. Doing what he could, he scrounged up some old clubs from his and our father's collection and managed to put together three mismatched sets that they could share.

One day he was playing golf with some people he didn't know and mentioned in the course of the conversation his golf team and their unusual equipment. The next Monday morning he was called down to the school office. One of the men he had played golf with over the weekend had shown up at the school with four complete sets of clubs, along with golf bags, wood covers, and three dozen new balls each.

My brother wanted to thank the man but didn't remember his name, so he wrote a letter to the local newspaper and it ran on the front page of the sports section. Within two weeks the school had received so much equipment they were able to donate several sets of clubs to other inner-city schools for their fledgling golf teams.

Tell them that, to ease them of their griefs,

Their fear of hostile strokes, their aches, losses,

Their pangs of love, with other incident throes

That nature's fragile vessel doth sustain

In life's uncertain voyage, I will some kindness do them.

—Shakespeare

It is impossible to pretend that you are not heir to, and therefore, however inadequately or unwillingly, responsible to, and for, the time and place that gave you life.

—James Baldwin

THE THAI MASSAGE

A friend of mine was traveling in Southeast Asia by herself. She's a very happily married woman in her mid-forties, and this was the adventure of a lifetime for her. While in Thailand she took advantage of their world-renowned foot massages. She was getting an especially luxurious massage one day (for $6.50, including a generous tip) and struck up a conversation with another solo traveler, a young man just out of college and backpacking his way around Asia. She decided to pay for his massage, too. Random acts of kindness, indeed.

●●●

Then cherish pity, lest
You drive an angel from your door

—William Blake

KEEPING WARM

It was the middle of winter and I had been driving around for weeks with a backseat full of old clothes to drop off at a local charity. For some reason, even though I drove past the collection point every day, I just kept forgetting to stop. One night after my shift had ended at midnight, I was driving home through downtown. The streets were deserted except for a man who was walking with just a blanket thrown over a thin cotton shirt to ward off the bitter cold.

I pulled a coat, down vest, and some gloves out of the pile in the backseat and, after driving a roundabout course to get through all the one-way streets, finally caught up with him. Jumping out of the car with the clothes, I ran up to him and said, "I hope they fit." I can still see the smile that spread across his lace as he thanked me. I hurried back to my warm car and I was smiling too, and a lot more thankful for all that I have to spare.

....

The white man knows
how to make everything
but he does not know how to distribute it.

—Sitting Bull

TEMPORARY CHECKS

I am a senior in high school and work at an athletic shoe store. One day a woman and her six-year-old son came in to buy school shoes. They found a pair he liked and came to the register to pay for them. As she was unfolding her checkbook I noticed they were temporary checks and I had to tell her that store policy would not let me accept her check.

Her son had been prancing around the store, testing out his new shoes and showing them to everyone; when she told him he had to take them off, tears started to well up in his eyes. It just broke my heart. I stopped him before he could untie them, and pulled out my checkbook and wrote a check for the shoes. His mother could not believe what I was doing. She wrote a temporary check out to me and gave me her address and telephone number so I would know that I could trust her.

As she walked out of the store she told me she would never forget me. It was not until later that I noticed she had made out the check for ten dollars more than the shoes cost. And at the bottom of the check on the memo line she had written: "For the nice woman at the shoe store."

CHRISTMAS SPIRIT

Many years ago my family spent the holidays in France. In the five days leading up to Christmas we had an increasingly depressing series of minor disasters. On Christmas Eve we checked into a dingy hotel in Nice with no holiday cheer in our hearts.

It was raining and cold when we went out for dinner. We ended up in a drab little restaurant. Inside only five tables were occupied, two German couples, two French couples, and an American sailor sitting by himself. In the corner a piano player listlessly played Christmas music. Everyone sat eating in stony silence; only the sailor seemed happy, writing a letter as he ate.

My wife ordered our meal in French. The waiter brought the wrong thing. I scolded my wife for being stupid and she began to cry. On our right one of the German wives began berating her husband. On our left a French father slapped his son for some minor infraction and the boy began to cry.

We were all interrupted by a blast of cold air as an old, thoroughly drenched French flower woman came in and made the rounds. But she had no takers. Wearily she sat down at a table and said to the waiter, "A bowl of soup. I haven't sold any flowers all afternoon." Then to the piano player she said, "Can you imagine, Joseph, soup on Christmas Eve?" He simply pointed to his empty tip jar.

The young sailor got up after finishing his meal, walked over to the flower woman, and, picking up two small corsages, said, "Happy Christmas, how much are these?" The woman told him two francs. He handed her a twenty-franc note, kissed her cheek, and said, "The rest is my Christmas present to you." He quickly walked to our table, handed one of the corsages to my wife, and departed.

For a moment the restaurant was completely silent. Then Christmas exploded like a bomb. The old flower woman jumped up doing a jig, and, waving the twenty-franc note, shouted to the piano player, "Joseph, my Christmas present! And you shall have half so you can eat, too."

The piano player began beating out "Good King Wenceslas," and my wife began to sing. Our children joined in, and the Germans jumped up on their chairs and began singing in German. The waiter embraced the flower woman, the French boy climbed onto his father's lap, and both joined in with the swelling international choir.

The Germans ordered wine for everyone, delivering it themselves along with hugs and Christmas greetings. One of the French families followed suit with Champagne and kisses. The owner of the restaurant began singing "The First Noel," and everyone joined in—half of us with tears in our eyes. People began crowding in from the street until the place was packed with diners while the Christmas songs rolled on.

Just minutes earlier, eighteen people were spending a miserable evening in the same room. It ended up with all of us sharing one of the very best Christmas Eves we had ever experienced—all because one young sailor held the Christmas spirit in his soul.

Without the human community one single human being cannot survive.

—The Dalai Lama

How rarely we weigh our neighbor in the same balance in which we weigh ourselves.

—Thomas à Kempis

The Baseball Mitt

When I was in college, I worked part time at a sporting goods store. There was a kid who would come by two or three times a week to visit this baseball mitt he wanted to buy. My manager and I would joke about him not only because he was so dedicated and persistent, but also because he had picked the best and most expensive mitt in the shop to be obsessed with.

This went on for months. The kid would come in, and you could tell he was so relieved that the mitt was still there. He would put it on, pound his fist into the pocket a couple of times, and then very carefully put it back onto the shelf and leave. Finally, one day he came in with a shoe box and a smile about eight miles wide and announced that he wanted to buy the mitt. So the manager brought the mitt over to the cash register while the kid counted out a shoe box worth of nickels, quarters, and dimes. His stash came to exactly $19.98.

The mitt cost $79.98, not including tax. My manager looked at the price tag, and sure enough the 7 was a little smudged, enough that a desperately hopeful seven-year-old could imagine it to be a 1. Then he looked at me, smiled, and very carefully recounted. "Yep, exactly $19.98." Wrapping up the mitt, he gave it to the boy.

Color in a Hospital

As a person with metastatic breast cancer, some days are filled with anxiety and fear, but then some "random" thing will happen which gives me a lift. There was the day in the cancer center when I sat across from a young man who was about to have blood drawn. He was of an age and thin in a way that suggested he might have AIDS. He sat with his eyes closed. I thought, his veins aren't what they once were and he's trying to help himself through this moment.

I felt a deep connection to this young man and I wanted to say "I love you," but I couldn't quite do it in that congested space where our knees almost touched and nurses threaded their way through the miniscule openings between patients. So I sat quietly, willing my "I love you" to reach him. Then my voice began to speak.

"I really like your colors," I said, "—those rich purple pants and your maroon tie-dyed socks that sing with them."

A smile stretched his thin lips and brought light to his face. "My socks match my under shirt," he said with a dash of impish pleasure.

"I see it peeking out beneath you shirt. It is a perfect match. And how the pants and tie-dye play together."

He opened his eyes and took me in. "And I like your turquoise. Oh, what a color!" We were living now in the fragile yet palpable world of our reflected colors. Suddenly, I saw freshly the only other visible colors in this white medical room.

"You can't see it, but your colors are drawing out their twins in the picture above your head," I told him.

His eyes focused above my head. "And your turquoise," he said, "is an extension of the sea in the picture over you."

His procedure ended. Our trance was broken, but I believe we flew together in our momentary world of colors.

....

Kind words can be short and easy to speak but their echoes are truly endless.

—Mother Teresa

THE GIANT OAK TREE

I had just graduated from college and had gone back to my hometown to visit friends. My parents had sold the family home a few years back and moved out of state, so I also took the opportunity to drive by the old house just to see it. Out in the front yard, perched in my giant oak tree, was a boy about ten years old. I stopped the car, went over to introduce myself, and told the boy that when I was his age I practically lived in that tree. He thought that was really funny because he said his mother was always telling people that he lives in that tree.

While we were standing there talking, laughing, and feeling very good about our shared tree, a car drove up to the curb right in front of us. A middle-aged man got out of the driver's side, came around to the passenger side, and helped a very frail-looking old man out of the car. I guess we were both staring, but the old man just walked right up to the tree, patted it on the side, looked at us, and said, "I planted this tree sixty years ago when there was nothing here but fields. I still like to come visit it now and then." Then he turned around, got back into the car, and drove away. We were both so shocked we didn't say a word until after the old man had left. Then the boy just looked at me and said, "Wow."

Complete possession is proved only by giving. All you are unable to give possesses you.

—Andre Gide

A hundred times every day I remind myself that my inner and outer life depends on the labors of other men, living and dead, and that I must exert myself in order to give in the measure as I have received and am still receiving.

—Albert Einstein

THE HAPPIEST OF PILGRIMS

Several years ago while walking the Camino de Santiago, a 500-mile pilgrimage trail across northern Spain, I met a young Iranian girl named Aamina. I first met her in the albergue—a kind of hostel for walkers—in the small town of Belorado. Her bunk was perpendicular to mine and she lay propped up for hours, barely moving. When she finally got up she surprised me by saying "excuse me" in English as she limped past. I asked what was wrong, and she explained that her foot was painfully infected. She was clearly distressed and had decided to take a bus to Burgos, the next major city, to find a doctor. Just watching her move was distressing. Yet the next morning I saw her limping her way to Burgos and thought "there's a tough kid."

A couple of days later, while exploring the old section in Burgos, I saw her waiting in line at the city albergue. She told me how she had walked to Villafranca in great pain and finally took a bus to Burgos. There, crying in pain— she had huge blisters and had lost a nail on an infected toe—she limped into the main plaza where she stood tearful and baffled. Unexpectedly someone touched her elbow and asked if she was a pilgrim. It was an older woman who asked what was wrong. After hearing her story the woman said, "I have a daughter about your age. You are my daughter today."

She took Aamina to lunch, then to the hospital to get her feet treated, then found her a hotel room and paid for it, telling her she would be back at seven to take her to dinner. When Aamina left the room to meet her new friend, she found a new pair of good walking shoes outside the door. The desk clerk said the women dropped the shoes off and left, not wanting Aamina to make a fuss. All she learned about the woman was she taught French in a university. The shoes fit well.

I walked with Aamina a short while the next morning. Her feet were better. She walked slowly and steadily, planning to cover about eleven miles that day. We were planning eighteen miles, so I moved on and did not see her again in the coming days. But the day after my arrival in Santiago, I met her on the street. We greeted with a hug. She was aglow, her dark eyes deep enough to drown in. I asked her how her feet were, and she gracefully swirled, hair and skirt awhirl. Hours later, after dinner, she once again greeted us in a narrow, crowded street—twirling, smiling Amine, the happiest of pilgrims.

Eyes Wide Open

We wanted to give our thirteen-year-old son a bigger view of the world. To this end, we moved to Japan and made plans to travel to Thailand on winter break. But we were troubled by one question: how could we justify spending money for airfare, hotel, food, and souvenirs when this impoverished third world country was still recovering from the aftermath of a devastating tsunami? Our solution was simple.

We gave our son a Christmas card with cash in it. The caveat was that he had to exchange the cash into baht and look for those who needed it more. To see need through a child's eyes was a powerful lesson that forever touched us.

As we were making our way through the crowded Chatuchak Weekend Market in Bangkok, I found myself getting annoyed in the crowded alleyway by a slow-moving line. As I cut across at the first opening I could find, I felt a tug on my elbow. "Look, Mom!" My gaze turned back to the cause of the congestion and found a blind man being led by his own young son through the twists and turns of the market. Without hesitation, my son made his way to the blind man's son; he leaned down and tucked a fistful of baht into his small hand. As their eyes met, no words needed to be spoken. In all honesty, this small act of kindness probably didn't alter the young son and father as much as it did our son. He received much more than he gave that day.

What wisdom can you find that is greater than kindness?

—Jean-Jacques Rousseau

We may have all come on different ships, but we're in the same boat now.

—Martin Luther King, Jr.

NATURE

There is a beautiful old spruce tree that grows in a field along the street to my home. For years it has been a comforting and serene part of my daily commute. Over the past few years I had watched a thick vine grow around the tree and climb its trunk. As time went by, the vine grew more and more vigorously, and the poor old tree was clearly suffering. I don't know why I simply observed and did nothing.

One Saturday morning as I was driving my children into town for assorted sporting events, I noticed an elderly couple had driven into the field and were rummaging around in their car. Returning home many hours later I saw the couple sweating away in the hot sun, doing mortal battle with the massive vine. I quickly changed into my yard clothes, mixed up a pitcher of lemonade, threw an assortment of fruit and snacks into a cooler, and headed over to the field.

When I got there I was astounded by what I saw: the couple had been hacking away for half the day already, and a huge pile of cut vines with stems as thick as a garden hose lay next to the tree. But there was much more to be done. I greeted the couple with my offerings, and after a brief, friendly picnic we all got back to the task at hand.

By the end of the day we had attracted three more volunteers, and by sunset you could almost hear a sigh of relief from that old spruce. Our efforts were not in vain; now whenever I drive past my heart fills with joy over the robust appearance of that beautiful tree.

It's the
Little Things:

Small Acts
That Make a
Big Impression

A gift consists not in what is done or given, but in the intention of the giver or doer.

—Seneca

Words of Comfort

I grew up in what we would now call a dysfunctional family. My parents materially were quite well off, but we lived amidst emotional chaos and confusion in a wealthy suburb of Philadelphia. As with most children, I simply assumed that this was the way it was and that the problems, the undercurrents of anger and hostility, were somehow my fault. One day when I was still very young, after a particularly painful and confusing series of interactions with my parents, our maid took me aside to talk to me. She told me that she did not care if it cost her her job, she just could not continue to be a silent observer. She told me that my parents were crazy, that they were acting badly, and not at all like good loving parents should act toward their children. She told me that I was a good, sweet girl and that the situation was not my fault. It must have taken a lot of courage for her to do that. Not only to overcome the natural hesitation to intervene between parents and children, but to take the risk that I would not say something about our talk to my parents. I never did talk about it. It was an incredible gift. Her words gave me the explanation I needed, a way to stop blaming everything on myself.

VERTIGO

I used to suffer from vertigo. My fear of heights was not something I ever anticipated; it would just come over me. I never gave it any thought until suddenly I found myself reeling with dizziness or paralyzed and unable to move. One day I was walking to an appointment when I came to an overpass. It wasn't even that high, but I could not cross it. I stood there feeling foolish and helpless. I wanted to keep my appointment, but there I was, frozen, unable to proceed.

A woman crossing from the opposite direction with her small son noticed me standing there in obvious distress and came over to me. "Are you all right?" she asked. "Oh, I feel so foolish," I said, "but I have a fear of heights and I can't cross this bridge." "Would it help if I crossed with you?" she asked. Taking my arm, she and her son walked back across the bridge with me. That happened twenty years ago, but I'll always remember that woman.

When I give I give myself.

—Walt Whitman

Kindness is more important than wisdom, and the recognition of this is the beginning of wisdom.

—Theodore Isaac Rubin

Kind Advice

The simplest acts of kindness can have such a powerful impact. Some years ago I was working through college selling children's books door to door in Florida. One particularly blistering day nothing was going right. I had knocked on every door without a single answer; I was hot, tired, and felt like a total failure. I wanted nothing more than to quit my job and run home to the Midwest. I wasn't thinking about selling books—I just wanted water and place to rest for a few minutes.

I looked down the street at a small white house and was drawn toward it. I had barely knocked on the door when an older woman opened it and immediately asked me in. She gave me a drink and invited me to share a meal with her and her husband. It was obvious that they did not have much money.

During the two hours I was there, the woman and her husband shared stories of the hardships and experiences in their lives and told me that it was very important to always love and care deeply about others—even strangers. As I left, the man gave me money and said he just wanted to help me out and that he had no need for my books. As I walked back down the street I broke into tears and sobbed for blocks. These people who at first seemed to have so little had given me more than I could ever have asked for.

OUT OF THE SILT

Tropical Storm Irene washed forty of a Vermont farmer's cows down the river and over a dam on August 24, 2011. In some places Irene's stifling silt goes down five feet. He was one of many farmers whose land either got covered over or slipped away in the worst flood since 1927. In some places people got twelve inches of rain in four hours. And now what's left of his soil is not only toxic, but hard as cement.

Still, one little patch of green showed through, near one of his few standing buildings.

My friend explained to me, "I'd just come to help muck out," a phrase all Vermonters quickly grew to understand as they donned masks and grabbed shovels and buckets. She told me the farmer had asked her, "Do you like delphiniums?"

My friend admitted to me she wasn't too sure what delphiniums were, but to him, she had said, "Oh, yes." The farmer took a little hoe and dug one up from the lone remaining patch of green. Then he handed it to her.

She planted it in her garden. Next spring, she will probably look at that little patch of azure, mirroring the sky, and think, "Out of the silt came this surprising thing." And from one who had lost so much, a great gift materialized.

THE GOOD FRIEND

A good friend and I had finally gotten together one evening after months of trying to coordinate our schedules and make the fifty mile drive separating us. We went out to eat and as usual had a great time talking about everything. I am always amazed at how quickly and deeply we reconnect even after months of barely speaking on the telephone.

While we were catching up on each other's lives, my friend noticed a man sitting alone at a table in the corner of the restaurant and commented to me that he looked sad, as if he were lacking for company. When we had finished our meal, I insisted on paying and my friend went along smiling. When the waiter came to pick up the check, my friend told him that she would like to pay—anonymously— for the dinner of the man in the corner. I realized again why I cared about her so much.

....

I keep my ideals, because in spite of everything I still believe that people are really good at heart.

—Anne Frank

NOTHING BUT NET

Anyone who has ever played basketball knows that playing with no net really takes some of the fun out of it. You just don't get that great whoosh feel when the ball drops straight through a naked hoop. But this didn't deter some teenage boys in our neighborhood who were regularly in their driveway, tossing the ball through an empty hoop. One day a neighbor they didn't know stopped in front of their house, rolled down the window, handed them a basketball net, called out "Merry Christmas!" and drove off. The boys just stood there staring at the net in their hands—but not for long! Every now and then they interrupt their game to wave at their new friend as he drives by. And then—*whoosh*—nothing but net.

....

What really matters is what you do with what you have.

—Shirley Lord

Just do what must be done. This may not be happiness, but it is greatness.

—George Bernard Shaw

I am larger, better than I thought. I did not know I held so much goodness.

—Walt Whitman

LITTLE THINGS

Being a hospice volunteer gives me the opportunity to come up with new ways to tell someone how special they are. And every once in a while, there's a chance to do something really fun.

A new ice cream parlor had opened in town, and my patient and her three elderly sisters wanted to hear the details. I promised that I'd treat everyone to ice cream on my next visit.

The day arrived, and it was a real scorcher. I grabbed my insulated bag and drove to Main Street Sweets, where I wrote a list of all the flavors and arrived at the sisters' house on schedule. Then I sat with each one, reading the list as they imagined each flavor until they made their decisions. One peppermint, one rum raisin, one butter pecan and one strawberry. I opted for butterscotch ripple.

Armed with my list, I went back to the ice cream store and bought double scoops all around. I loaded up my bag and raced back to the house, hoping the ice cream wouldn't melt. I handed out the containers and each sister complained that I'd bought too much, that they could never eat so much ice cream. But one bite led to the next, as it often does with ice cream, and before long, there wasn't a bite left. There was giggling and delight, and for that moment, the room was filled with a giddy bunch of schoolgirls enjoying the cool of an ice cream on a mid-summer's day.

Now, months later, as the snow swirls outside my window, the ice cream and two of the sisters are long gone. But the sound of their laughter and the image of our ice cream party on that sweltering day will be a part of my mind's landscape for as long as I live.

. . . .

When it comes to getting things done, we need fewer architects and more bricklayers.

—Colleen C. Barrett

SHADE AT A MAGIC SHOW

When I was twelve years old, I ended up in a Shriner's hospital in a full body cast, lying flat on my back for six months. I was surrounded by wonderful people doing everything they could to help me. One particular Sunday we had a scheduled picnic outdoors, and all the kids were brought outside for hamburgers, hot dogs, and a magic show.

My bed was wheeled outside, but by time the magic show was about to start I found myself staring right into the sun, forcing me to close my eyes. Suddenly the sun seemed to disappear, and I opened my eyes to find a Shriner purposefully standing in a position that completely blocked the sun and still allowed me to see the stage. He stood there for the entire hour of the show—directly in line with the sun and shading his eyes with his hand.

This happened many years ago, but I have never forgotten what that man did to allow a little girl to witness the magic of magic and the magic of kindness.

COMPETITIVE KINDNESS

When I was in high school, I started playing field hockey. Since this was on the West Coast, there were no organized men's leagues, and we would more often than not end up playing college teams or adult club teams. One day we played the local university team, which included one of the best field hockey players in the country. They killed us. I remember running around like mad, exerting massive amounts of energy while this one guy just glided around, past, and through us to score whenever he wanted. After the game I was sitting on the ground trying to catch my breath when the star walked over and started talking to me. For a while he just talked, going into all the intricacies of the game; he spoke to me as if I were an equal, as if I already understood all the things he was saying. After I had finally caught my breath, he took me back out on the field and spent an hour showing me various moves and tactics. I know it sounds silly, but even though the words were all about field hockey, the feeling it gave me was so much larger.

A Simple Compliment

I did not go through my teenage years gracefully. I was overweight and pear-shaped with glasses, braces, and acne. My self-consciousness was aggravated by my little sister, who was ten years younger than me and so pretty. She had apple cheeks and long auburn ringlets, and people would stop us on the street just to admire her. One day one of my mother's friends, whom I adored because she was so sophisticated and stylish and because she always treated me as a person rather than a child, complimented me on my eyebrows. She told me that they were so dark and beautifully shaped that they made me look very exotic. Forty years later that single compliment—given so freely and sincerely to a child who did not feel at all attractive or exotic—still fills my heart with gratitude.

* * *

Five things constitute perfect virtue: gravity, magnanimity, earnestness, sincerity, and kindness.

—Confucius

Courageous Kindness

An act of kindness can sometimes take incredible courage. I was at the county fair many years ago with my mother. I remember it was a very, very hot day and all around us children and parents were melting down. We were walking behind a woman with two small children. The children were crying and whining and the mother was getting increasingly upset. Finally she started to scream at them to shut up; then she turned around and struck them both very hard. Seeing this happen right in front of me made me feel like I had been hit as well.

Of course her kids starting crying even more, and the mother was on the verge of completely losing control when my mother walked up to her, touched her arm, and said something like, "You poor dear, don't worry, sometimes things just get out of control for a moment." Then my mother offered to take the children over to the ice cream stand and sit with them while the woman took a little walk to compose herself. She returned in about ten minutes, thanked my mother, hugged her children, and went on.

BETTER THAN MEDICINE

The contractions came on quickly. I got to the hospital without incident, only to find that my doctor was not around. This was my third child, and the labor was rapid and intense. For three hours the contractions built and still my obstetrician had not shown up. It was pretty obvious that this child wasn't going to wait. One of the interns (I never saw her) stood behind me and began stroking my cheek. Such a simple act.

That was thirty-one years ago and the memory has stayed with me ever since. There in the midst of the daily business of a hospital, some wonderful person reached out to a scared woman in pain, stroked her cheek, and gave a gift of human comfort that has lasted for so many years.

AUTOMOTIVE ANGEL

For many years, our next-door neighbor was this very sweet and unusual old woman. Her husband had died quite young, and she had lived alone ever since her children grew up and moved out. When my brother and I were young, she always treated us as real people, not just a couple of kids. She would talk to us seriously about what was happening in our lives, and actually took an interest in things like the wins and losses of our baseball teams. She also had what at the time was a really hot car—a silver 1957 Chevy—that she took great care of. As she got older, her son took over the duties of occasionally washing and polishing the car, but then he moved out of state.

One day my brother and I were at our parents' house for Thanksgiving dinner and we noticed that her poor old Chevy was looking very sad. Later that night we snuck into her driveway, washed the car inside and out, waxed it, and polished all the chrome; when we were done it was shining just like a floor model.

That was nearly five years ago, and since then we have made regular guerrilla raids into her driveway. I don't think she knows who is doing it, but my mother reports that she has taken to going "cruising" in her car, and always laughs and tells my mother she has an "automotive angel."

SEEING THE SKY

I live high in the hills and my body is getting old. One day I was out in my garden fussing with weeds and grew tired. I decided to lie back on the grass and rest like I used to when I was a small boy. I woke up some minutes later with a neighbor whom I had never met leaning over me, all out of breath, asking me if I was okay. He had looked out his window two blocks up the hill and saw me lying on my back on the grass, looking, I am sure, like the victim of a stroke or heart attack, and had run all the way down the hill to check on me. It was embarrassing but it was also so wonderfully touching. After we had it all sorted out, he let out a deep breath and lay down on the grass beside me. We both stayed there very quietly for a while and then he said, "Thank you for deciding to take your nap out on the lawn where I could see you. The sky is such a beautiful thing and I cannot remember the last time I really looked at it."

THE MENTOR

It was a blustery day in Pasadena, California. The year was 1970. I had just started the second quarter of my first year in the seminary. Sitting in Greek class one evening I realized I had to quit; I had no heart for the study of classic languages and philosophical theology. The next morning, amid the protestations of the registrar and my adviser, I filled out the forms to drop out of graduate school. I had been doing very well and no one understood why I was leaving. But I felt increasingly clear about the rightness of the decision.

As I was walking from the registrar's office to the library, I passed the office of one of my professors. He was sitting at his desk, noticed my passing, and called me into his office. He saw the forms I was carrying and inquired about what I was doing. I shared with him my decision to drop out, and he very graciously responded with his disappointment and his blessing. Then he said something that eventually changed my life. Very kindly he remarked, "You are a talented young man with a future in theology, and even if you don't decide to go into the ministry, I think you should come back to complete your degree someday." I thanked him and walked out, quite touched by his kindness.

His prophecy came true. I returned two years later, completed my degree, found my way into theological publishing, and eventually the professor who had been so kind to me became one of my bestselling authors.

PAYBACK

I had an older neighbor who was very kind to me, a father figure really. After he died, I noticed that his yard had become completely overgrown; his widow was not physically able to do the gardening. So one morning, after I saw her leave for the day, I jumped the fence and put in a few hours of work. It was my way of paying him back for the care he had taken of me.

....

Love has nothing to do with what you are expecting to get—only what you are expecting to give.

—Katharine Hepburn

TEAM BONDING

I was the new kid at my high school, and, being very shy, I found it hard to make friends. My escape was volleyball. I love to play and was good enough to get on the girls' varsity team. Most of the girls on the team were pretty nice, but they had been playing together for three years and I was clearly the outsider. The third game of the season was our biggest challenge; we had to play the state champions, and they had an absolutely awesome player on their team named Angela.

We knew we didn't have much of a chance at winning, but we at least wanted to play well. I think I played okay, but I don't remember doing anything that special. Anyway, we lost, but we forced the match to go to three games and were even ahead for a little while. When we were collecting our stuff after the game, Angela walked up, pointed her finger right at me, and said, "You are good, girl!" Then she smiled and walked away.

I was so surprised I was almost embarrassed until my whole team came running over to hug me. On the way back to the bus, one of my teammates turned to me and said, "Next year we'll beat them, because Angela is graduating and we've still got you."

THE MYSTERY DECORATOR

My folks are currently living at a retirement community in Massachusetts. Each apartment has a shelf to the right or left of the door, where the occupants display holiday decorations, special mementos, and other attractive items to make the corridors bright and cheerful. People often change their shelves with the seasons as well. There seems to be a "mystery decorator" who will add a special item to the shelf of a person who is ill or decorate a shelf that looks incomplete or empty. When my mother was in the hospital recently, she returned to find a lovely violet plant on her shelf—one of her favorites actually. This "mystery decorator" does not leave any notes or any clues—just spreads anonymous joy and surprises to the residents.

....

I don't know what your destiny will be, but one thing I do know: the only ones among you who will be really happy are those who have sought and found how to serve.

—Albert Schweitzer

GIFT KITTEN

My son is wheelchair-bound from a head injury he suffered in an accident last year. He recently decided he wanted a kitten to keep him company and started watching the classified ads in the local paper. An ad finally appeared, and after calling to make sure there were still kittens available, I drove across town to pick one up for him. When I got there I found the last kitten cuddled up in the arms of a young man named Ron.

I was disappointed because I knew how excited my son was, and it must have shown on my face. I told the young man my story, and he graciously smiled, handed me the kitten, and told me not to worry—he would find another one. As I sit and watch the joy on my son's face when he plays with that little black-and-white cat, I can't help but think of that wonderfully generous young man.

Tree Climbing

One day when I was a senior in high school, I was walking home from school and noticed an elderly couple standing at the base of a very tall pine tree. They were looking up and yelling and were obviously very upset. I thought that maybe their cat had gotten stuck in the tree, and since I had spent many of my best times as a young boy climbing trees, I went to see if I could help.

At the top of the tree was a very young girl. She couldn't have been more than three or four years old. Apparently she was staying with her grandparents and, when they weren't looking, she had shimmied up the tree. They had already called the fire department, but I felt like I should at least climb up far enough so that if she started to fall I might be able to catch her. When I got within a few feet of the little girl, she gave me this huge smile and said hi.

I almost started laughing because she was not at all scared; in fact she looked as at ease as a monkey on its home branch. We ended up talking for a while about how great it felt to climb trees, and as we talked, cradled in that pine tree, I could feel my whole body relaxing into the tree. I had this wonderful feeling that everything was just right with the world.

Then she said, "We better go down now," and, as we climbed down the tree (I was very careful to keep myself close and below her), I could see that she was never in any real danger. She moved as though she could scramble up and down that tree a million times and never come close to slipping. As I walked home, I realized that that was the first time I had crawled out onto the limb of a tree in many, many years. The thought made me want to go back and thank that little girl.

. . . .

The best and most beautiful things in the world cannot be seen or even touched.

They must be felt with the heart.

—Helen Keller

A Closet Full of Coats

I had an hour to eat before I presented to dozens of hearty souls willing to come out to a bookstore event in freezing cold.

Three blocks away I finished dinner and pulled on a calf-length wool coat. More snow flurries had begun. I pushed the door open and the chill slapped my face. As I turned, I noticed a woman sitting on a square of cardboard. Her pale skin showed above her tennis shoes and ankle socks. She was wearing a short, thin jacket. I checked my watch. Ten minutes to my start time. I walked on.

Live Boldly was the basis of my presentation. I paged through the life philosophies outlined in my book. As my steps slowed, I was filled with whispers of objections, all telling me I couldn't go back, that I didn't have time, that I'd catch cold.

I thought of the many coats in my closet at home. The woman was startled by my quick approach. Scared.

"Do I have to move?" She asked.

"I need you to stand up," I said. She complied.

I took my coat off and helped her into it. She was a slip of a thing so it easily wrapped around her windbreaker. Tears of relief slipped down the slopes of her cheeks.

I buttoned her coat. I adjusted her collar. I patted her shoulders and said, "Can you find someplace warm tonight?"

She nodded that she could.

I walked in the falling snow—warmed by the inextinguishable flame of an unexpected, practical kindness. I didn't look back. When I arrived at the bookstore I was surprised that I didn't feel the chill of the storm at all.

* * *

I am only one; but still I am one.

I cannot do everything, but still I can do something.

I will not refuse to do the something I can do.

—Helen Keller

The Answering Machine

Who would ever think that a telephone answering machine could change your life? I had just left a long and very painful relationship and found myself suddenly in a new city without friends, anything to do, and any desire to find either. I was like a listless blob of expended energy. Every day I would come home from work and just stare at the walls, sometimes crying, but mostly just sitting and wondering if this cloud would ever go away.

I had bought an answering machine—why, I don't know, since nobody ever called me. One night I came home and the red light was flashing. I couldn't believe it, a phone call! When I played it back, a wonderful male voice started to apologize for calling the wrong number, and I burst into tears. But then he kept talking. He said my voice on the message had sounded so sad and he just wanted to tell me that it was okay to be sad, that being able to feel that sadness was important. His message went on for almost twenty minutes, just talking about how important it was to be able to go through the pain instead of running away from it, and how even though it probably seemed impossible now, things would get better. He never even said his name, but that message was, in a very important way, the beginning of my life.

Love is not getting, but giving. Not a wild dream of pleasure and a madness of desire—oh, no—love is not that! It is goodness and honor and peace and pure living—yes, love is that and it is the best thing in the world and the thing that lives the longest.

—Henry van Dyke

THE OUT OF THE BLUE PHONE CALL

In 1993, shortly after obtaining my master's degree in counseling, I was the recipient of an anonymous random act of kindness that forever changed my life. At the time, I was enjoying my work at Community Mental Health, yet I couldn't shake a strong internal draw to enter into private practice.

Through my own healing journey, I had learned several holistic, alternative methods that were providing life-changing healing results for me and for many others as well. By offering these alternative methods in a private practice, I could provide the same opportunity for people who desired more than traditional counseling. The dilemma for me at the time was financial; this move would have been risky without some form of safety net.

That all changed with one out of the blue phone call. I was surprised when the case manager from a local agency that served children and families in adoptive and foster care situations asked if I would be willing to sub-contract with them to help these families. When I inquired as to how she knew about me, she said I had come highly recommended by a friend of her superior. She didn't know who that friend was. This phone call offered enough security for me to take the leap. It felt like such a miracle and an answer to my prayers.

This rewarding work allowed me to help many children heal from the pains of the past and move forward with dignity and a sense of strength. Since this sub-contract work was part time, I was able to expand my practice by writing self-healing books and offering individual appointments and classes on a sliding scale or at no cost to those in need.

I have asked around and asked around, and still, twenty years later, this angel of kindness is anonymous. I love how just one simple act ripples out to become many more.

The Water Heater

Years ago I had to have a new water heater installed. A very surly man showed up to do the installation, giving short, curt answers to my every question. I thought he was simply a sour old man and left him to his work.

When he finished, he said he had to wait for another worker to arrive to help him carry the old tank out of my basement. I invited him to sit in my kitchen and offered him some coffee. He said "nope," and just sat down at my table with legs and arms crossed. I rolled my eyes and went about my work, knowing he'd be gone soon.

After a few moments he asked what was flashing on my dining room table. I retrieved a small clock shaped like a computer workstation and gave it to him to look at. I explained how it used solar power to alternately flash the time and the name of my company. He said "hmmph," and set it on the kitchen table, but I noticed he continued to look at it from time to time.

Finally his assistant came, and they carried the tank from the basement. He returned to my back door to get my signature, and I asked him to wait. I went in and got the clock and said, "Here, take this with you." He said, "Are you serious?" I said yes and smiled, and he nodded and started to leave. He hesitated, turned back to me, and said, "ya know, my wife died six weeks ago, and this is the first nice thing anyone's done for me." He looked at me one last moment, the corners of his mouth barely turning up, and walked away.

I walked back into my kitchen and broke down crying.

SUMMER CAMP

When I was ten years old I went to summer camp for the first time. That school year had been very difficult for me. For reasons I never understood, I had become the girl everyone loved to tease. I was isolated, called names, and even beat up as I walked home from school. But I was excited about summer camp and vowed to make everyone there like me.

Well, it happened again. Three days in at camp, and a couple of girls snuck into my suitcase while I was in the shower and threw my underwear all over the cabin. The counselors did their best to console m,e but I was hysterical and couldn't understand why everyone hated me.

A couple nights later at one of our campfire sing-alongs, I was sitting alone. I enjoyed singing, and we were doing this beautiful John Denver song that really comforted me. I sat there singing quietly to myself when an older camper from California came over and asked if she could sit by me. It made me feel so special. Here was this older girl who wanted to sit by me!

They were handing out awards that night and I was hoping for the "Songbird" award that went to the best singer at camp. When it went to another girl who happened to sing much louder than I did, I was devastated. Then my new friend sitting beside me announced to everyone, "Angela has a beautiful voice too!" It felt so good to have someone give me a compliment in front of everyone. She also told me she wanted to sit next to me because she loved to hear me singing and thought I was the nicest girl at camp.

I don't remember her name, and I never saw her again after that summer, but I know I never thanked her properly for the wonderful kindness she showed to me.

TRUE CONNECTION

I am sixteen years old and still learning about who I am and how to live. One weekend I went with a boyfriend to his family reunion. I felt very uncomfortable and didn't know what to say. I ended up sitting next to his grandfather. He started to tell me all about his late wife, their first date, engagement, and marriage, and their last days together. He spoke with such genuine feeling that for two hours I laughed and cried and was completely captured by his incredible stories. By the time I had to go it felt like I was sitting next to a close friend, and I was reluctant to leave this man who had entrusted me with such precious memories and had made me feel so included. I broke up with my boyfriend shortly afterward, but I will never forget that conversation.

....

It's the small things that are hard to do.

—John B. Flannagan

THE BUS DRIVER WITH HEART

While riding the bus to work one day, I noticed a small boy—no more than six or seven—board the bus. I was surprised that no adult accompanied him. With an oversized backpack on his back, it was obvious he was on his way to school, and he asked the driver to call out his stop. He sat so adult-like in the front of the bus. I watched as his small legs dangled off the seat, unable to reach the floor. The bus driver called out his stop and waited patiently while the boy attempted to cross the busy street. Cars continued to whiz by. Then the driver put on the emergency brake, stepped off the bus, and took the boy's hand to lead him across the street. My heart filled with emotion. As I was leaving I got the driver's name and wrote a letter to the transit company, thanking them for having such a wonderful employee.

Duckling Rescue

Twenty-five years ago, I was riding in a taxicab in Amsterdam and saw a mother duck crossing the street ahead of us with a long line of ducklings waddling behind her. The cab driver never even attempted to slow down; he just plowed through them. It was a sickening moment, and even though it happened so long ago I can still feel the wrenching in my stomach every time I see ducks walking. The healing balm for that memory finally showed up today in a tiny story in my local newspaper:

> She paced anxiously back and forth like a nervous basketball coach at a crucial game. If she had hands, she would have been wringing them nonstop. But she didn't. She was a duck. A duck with a lot at stake, no less. During a morning waddle across Fallen Leaf Circle in San Ramon Thursday, her five tiny ducklings had slipped between the two-inch slit in a storm-drain grate.
>
> Cars passed and people walked by, but neither man nor vehicle nor Animal Control could sway her from her post. At last, rescue arrived. Out of nowhere, four burly guys from Public Works and Animal Control Services— one or two who looked like they'd treat a duck about as gently as a bowling ball—unbolted the grate and stepped tenderly down the drain so they didn't scare the little fellas.

One of them scooped up the ducklings and set them down in a white plastic bucket, cradling each one like a precious gem. They poured the ducklings into a nearby creek and the little family was last seen paddling off into the sunrise.

WORDS OF COMFORT

I was walking up Amsterdam Avenue in New York during a particularly dark time of my life. I had recently lost a lover, and the pressures of law school were gaining on me. The darkness in my heart must have come to the surface, because as I walked by a destitute street person he turned to me and said, "It can't be that bad." Simple words that changed my life and brought the spirit back to my form.

....

What we give to the poor is what we carry with us when we die.

—Peter Marin

A VERY KIND BOY

A few years ago I had managed to screw up my life so badly that I found myself without a home and without hope. I'm ashamed to admit it, but even then I was so absorbed by my own self-pity that all I could think of was begging enough money to buy the cheapest drink I could find. One day I was sitting in front of a store panhandling when a woman walked by with a small boy in tow. She ignored my pitch and hurried away. As I watched them go down the sidewalk, the small boy broke free and came running back. He stood in front of me, fumbling in his coat pocket, and pulled out a five-dollar bill and handed it to me. That was almost certainly more money than he had ever held before,

I was completely dumbstruck and just sat there staring at him with the money in my hand. By then his mother had returned, and with tears in her eyes she gently led the boy away. He turned back once to wave and they were gone. I don't know how long I sat there, but I have not had another drink since then.

In Need of a Hug

W hen I was six years old my mother took me to school on opening day. Sometime during that first day, a small boy started to cry. I immediately went over to him and put my arms around him. The teacher ordered me to return to my assigned seat. I could not believe this teacher's indifference toward this boy, because whenever I cried at home some member of my family would be right there with their arms around me.

My teacher kept telling me to leave the boy alone, and I kept refusing to obey her until eventually the boy stopped crying. I went home that day with a note to my mother stating that I was rude, disobedient, and a troublemaker. I explained to my mother just what had happened, and she came back to school with me the next day. She told my teacher that I had been taught to be considerate and caring toward others and that I was not likely to change. She strongly advised my teacher to get used to my sympathetic nature.

That incident happened seventy-two years ago, and I have enjoyed hugging a lot of troubled people since then.

WEEPING WILLOWS

When I was in high school, I had a friend who asked me to help him plant some weeping willow trees down by a creek. It seems that he had watched every year as the banks of this creek had been increasingly eaten away. It had gotten to the point where the water was threatening to overflow into the nearby housing development. My friend had obviously done his research; he found out that willows grew quickly, easily, and with a great spreading root system that drinks up lots of water, which would stabilize the creek hank. When I met him at the creek, he had a huge bundle of willow branches in his arms. We spent most of the day planting these willow sprigs up and down the endangered curve.

Many years later, I was home visiting and found myself walking down by that creek. Where we spent that afternoon is now a beautiful idyllic bend with a long curving row of large graceful willows bending out over the water.

ON THE BUS

I ride the bus to and from work every day—it's about a thirty-five-minute trip. When you commute like I do, you have a real appreciation for the difference between sitting down, which allows you to either doze off or read and just relax, and standing up, during which you are constantly being tossed to one side or another, trying not to smash into other standees and constantly moving out of the way so people can get on or off. It makes you develop a keen sense of strategy for getting a seat. I've discovered that if I cut across the hill a few blocks to catch the bus earlier in its route, it greatly increases my odds of finding a seat. There is one elderly woman who is pretty much on the same schedule as I am, and before my discovery I used to get on the bus and she would already be there—usually seated while I remained standing. After my discovery, she would get on the bus and sometimes end up standing while I was already seated. It made me feel a little odd, like I had somehow cheated her, but I did not give up my seat.

One day coming back from work I was standing on the bus when I was suddenly hit by this wave of nausea. I felt like I was going to pass out, but I was trying very hard not to make a scene. Suddenly I felt a hand on my arm guiding me down into a seat. It was the woman from my morning bus whom I almost never saw going back. Very gently she helped me into what had been her seat and then hovered over me in a wonderfully protective way to give me some privacy to disappear in. By the time we got back to our neighborhood, I felt well enough to thank her and get home. Ever since that day, I always give her my seat in the morning; in fact, I look forward to it.

The Skiing Accident

When I was about nineteen or twenty, I was skiing down a mountain when I saw a woman who had fallen. She was clearly hurt and crying and trying to get up, but she couldn't. So I flagged down somebody to get the ski patrol and stayed with her, talking to her, holding her hand, touching her shoulder. It was the last run of the day; it was getting really cold and snowing hard. About a half hour later, the ski patrol showed up and took her down the mountain. I stayed with her because she was so scared. She kept saying, "I think there might be something wrong." I said, "Well there might be. I'll make sure you get the care you need." Finally the ambulance came and took her to the hospital. I guess her leg was broken in about four places. I never saw her again, but it was clear my presence was important to her. I know that's true.

A Discarded Trundle Bed

A few years ago, I made the heartbreaking decision to end my marriage of eight years and move out on my own. I had no money at the time, and a friend offered me the vacant bedroom in his apartment while I got on my feet again. I had to be very selective about the things I could use in this very small space, though, because I needed to consider my young son, who would be staying with me several nights a week. The queen-size bed I already owned was not a practical choice, and I began looking through the want ads for a used trundle bed, so I could get two beds for the space of one. Asking prices ranged from $100 to $200 for the nice ones. Cheaper ones seemed to be gone by the time I picked up the phone.

One day I spoke to a good friend about my frustration and resignation about sleeping on the floor for a while. It just so happened that a wooden trundle bed was sitting on her front porch, a recent discard by one of the neighboring tenants. I picked it up that afternoon, and my son and I slept on it peacefully for months.

A New Pair of Socks

I was riding home from work on a crowded bus one day and found myself sitting next to an eight-year-old boy. He began singing quietly to himself, and as I listened I realized that he was singing his own song: "Today is my birthday, no one knows that it's my birthday, today is my birthday." I looked at him and said, "Is today really your birthday?" He got a big smile on his face and said yes. Then he started to cry and told me that he lived with his mother but that she wouldn't even remember it was his birthday because she was on drugs.

He told me that last year his teacher had given him a pair of socks for his birthday and that was the best present he ever had. I wanted to give him something, but when I looked into my purse all I had was $6.25 and I needed $1.25 for my next bus. So I gave him the five-dollar bill and said, "I want you to go buy yourself something just for your birthday." He looked at me and thanked me, saying he would never forget this birthday. As he was getting off at his stop, he turned back and smiled at me and said, "I'm going to go buy myself some socks."

Everyone Deserves a Break

The woman bus driver for the morning commute downtown had a reputation for being crusty and unpleasant. One morning a very pretty teenage girl got on the bus. In a matter of moments everyone on the bus was gagging—the girl smelled terrible and appeared to be completely unaware of it. Every morning for a week the girl would get on the bus and riders would open windows, scurry to get off, and even make cruel comments.

One day our bus driver took control. As the girl was waiting to get off at her stop, the driver leaned over and spoke very softly to her. She said she knew she was doing the best she could and that she knew how it felt to be left out because she was different; then she gave the girl some specific hygiene suggestions. The next day she gave her a small bag full of assorted toiletries and even offered to buy her some new underwear when the girl told her she didn't have any. The bus driver really touched something in this youngster and all of us regular passengers saw empathy and kindness in our bus driver that we had never noticed before.

Now we all treat the young girl with much more kindness, and I called the transit authority to tell them how courteous, safe, and helpful our driver is. If by any chance she has anything amiss in her personnel file, I wanted to at least balance that and give her a break, just as she went out of her way to give that girl a break.

KINDNESS STORIES FROM SUPERSTORM SANDY

WHEN NEIGHBORS AND STRANGERS JUMP IN TO HELP

"Come in," she said,
"I'll give you shelter from the storm."

—Bob Dylan

What Many Hands Can Do

It is hard to describe the depth and breadth of the debris that washed up in my riverfront yard during the storm that pummeled the New Jersey coast. One sailboat was impaled on a dumpster, another was wedged between two trees, and the beach clubs from Sea Bright, a barrier beach town just four blocks away, were completely destroyed. Two whole cabanas—room-sized buildings filled with refrigerators and furniture—and at least four smashed up ones, telephone poles, floating docks, and whole sets of stairs were in my yard. We took what we could to the curb and then waited for our insurance agent, who never came but just told us over the phone that they don't cover that kind of debris removal, only the removal of objects from inside the home.

We got two estimates for the clean-up costs—one was $20,000 and the other was $7,000. We were overwhelmed just thinking about it. On Sunday, nearly a week after the storm, we came home and saw that our neighbor who had had a similar situation was all clear. She said volunteers had done it; high school kids and some residents had formed a group and were going house to house up and down our street. I said no way, ours was too much and too big. Then this little kid no more than ten years old appeared and said, my dad can do it, he has a chainsaw.

My hopeful husband, Keith, stayed home the next day, and sure enough, about fifty people streamed into our yard and started carrying the debris out to the curb. The guy with the chainsaw was not there (he had to go to work that day), but we had the Rumson-Fair Haven Regional High School basketball coach and his seven-year-old daughter, the wife of a town councilman, and a slew of students, boys and girls. Keith had a sledgehammer, and he started to smash up a cabana so they could get it to the street. Then a neighbor came over with three more sledgehammers, and Keith and four freshmen—he kept saying it like that—freshmen—all took turns until they finished them off. It was amazing to see what many hands working together can do. They miraculously cleared everything away.

AN EARTH ANGEL

Newark, New Jersey's mayor, Cory Booker, is one of those angels on earth. He drove around Newark before, during, and after the storm, urging residents to be safe and remain inside. He even helped relocate homeless people to new shelters.

His Tools Were His Livelihood

My father was watching the news of the devastation in the New York area from his home in Bucks County, Pennsylvania. He was particularly saddened by the story of a Staten Island man who had his tools stolen during some looting that took place at his home. It turns out the man knew the two people who committed the crime.

These tools were all the man had to do his work and provide income for his family. Now, his home was destroyed and he had nothing.

My father looked up the man's name on the Internet, found who he hoped was him, and sent him a check to do with whatever he pleased. He's hoping it will be enough to buy a new set of tools.

I was particularly gladdened by my father's action, though it came as no surprise to me. (By the way, my father did not tell me of this, my mother did—and asked me not to tell anyone.)

LONG LINES MAKE FOR FAST FRIENDS

I was in the East Village when Sandy hit, and in the days that followed people seemed to really band together and help each other out. While the power, heat, and water were being restored, people in the neighborhood still wanted to get out and about. I've never seen such demand for coffee in my life. Food trucks running on generators served hot coffee and tacos, many pizzerias stayed open, and bartenders opened their doors to the public, tending bar with headlamps and making change the best they could.

Cash was a necessity during that time, and one night I was standing in a long ATM line uptown. The man in front of me tried to make a deposit, but the machine froze before mid- transaction, after he'd inserted the check. He seemed really stressed. The lady who was using the ATM next to him finished her transaction and turned to him and asked if she could help. They couldn't get the machine to unfreeze, the bank was closed, and the man explained he needed the deposit to go through to be able to withdraw cash. The lady asked how much he needed, and he said just twenty dollars. She didn't even hesitate about offering to loan him the money, saying, "I'll give you my business card, and when things are back to normal you can call me up and pay me back." This kind of attitude seemed to be all over New York that week—there was really a feeling that we're all in this together.

BUCKET BRIGADES AND BAKE SALES

Westbeth Artists' Housing, established in 1970 in New York City's West Village, provides affordable living and working spaces for artists and their families, many of them low income and seniors. The building was badly damaged in Hurricane Sandy; there was no electricity or running water for a week, and no heat for much longer than that because flooded boilers would take weeks to replace. There are over three hundred apartments on eleven floors, and there was no elevator service.

While some residents relocated or were able to stay with friends or family elsewhere, many remained. The building organized bucket brigades to deliver water up the flights of stairs for toilet flushing and washing, and volunteers passed out food and water to the residents.

Nearby, elementary school PS3 was shuttered for a week with the loss of power. Once school resumed, the parents and students were thinking about how they could help those affected by the storm. A call went out and supplies came pouring in, along with drivers to take the students and the supplies to the Rockaways, New Jersey, and Coney Island.

Thoughts turned to PS3's Election Day bake sale, and they decided to have proceeds benefit the Westbeth just four blocks away. Cookies and brownies and cakes flew off the table at the event, and sales topped $700. Parents took the money straight to a store and delivered piles of electric blankets to residents the same day. A week later, with the power back on but still no running water, residents couldn't use space heaters because of the fire risk. Sleeping warm was a pressing need, and the delivery brought tears to the eyes of the doorman on duty.

Meanwhile, across the country in San Francisco, a well-known publisher of cookbooks wanted to do something. They too decided on a bake sale. The company matched the proceeds and several thousand dollars were donated to the relief fund.

SURFING TO SAFETY

I think I read this on the *Huffington Post* website. A guy in Far Rockaway, New York, a neighborhood in Queens that was hardest hit by the storm, got his eighty-two-year-old mother to safety on his surfboard! He pulled her for several blocks to his brother's house on higher ground. Then he rescued his fifteen-year-old son. Then, he went to one of the streets where homes were still burning and helped a neighbor's mother to safety by getting her into a kayak and walking her out of harm's way.

I also heard about a bunch of guys, including one in his eighties, who formed a human chain and trudged through the water, keeping a firm grip on their neighbors to make sure everyone was okay. I heard there was a woman with a newborn baby and a pregnant woman, too.

SIXTEEN PILOTS READY TO HELP

I read this in the paper this afternoon and thought, wow, people are amazing. The owner of FCA Flight Center in Fitchburg, Massachusetts, organized a clothing drive for those in need after Superstorm Sandy and flew the supplies to Long Island's Republic Airport. What he never expected is that sixteen pilots showed up to help get the donations to people in need. As of this writing, just a week after the storm, he was organizing another trip this weekend.

....

HELP FROM ACROSS THE COUNTRY

I live in LA and sent some money for the storm victims through the Red Cross. But I was so proud of my neighbors who work for Southern California Edison. A bunch of them flew to New York to help restore electrical power in New York and New Jersey. Apparently they were given a real hero's welcome, too. One hundred and twenty employees from SCE and seventy trucks were flown to the scene to help. I hear this happened across the country, too.

DOOR-TO-DOOR HELP FOR THE ELDERS

I don't live in the area affected by Sandy, but I heard this incredible story on the radio. A guy—I think he lived in Atlantic City or somewhere on the Jersey Shore—decided to ride out the storm at home. He was working at his computer when he started feeling water under his shoes. His place was flooding fast. He said he opened his bedroom door and faced a wall of water about four feet high. He had to get out fast. I think he said he was staying in a shelter. But he and his sons went back to his street every day to make sure his neighbors were okay, especially the many old people who could no longer get around. He made sure they were still taking their medications and had food and water. What a sweetheart. I mean, he'd lost everything but he kept thinking about his neighbors.

Afterword

Take a deep breath and read the news, watch TV, look around. Dependence on oil is slow suicide. Clean water dwindles. Polar ice caps crumble. Whole animal species vanish in a dying breath. The air, the water, the earth—the foundations of our world—seem in shorter supply than ever. The walls are closing in.

So why am I optimistic? Is looking on the bright side some stubborn weed I'd do better to pull up at the root? Is blind faith binding me to a poisonous fate? No. I'm optimistic, cautiously, realistically, and partly because I cannot help but be bowled over by kindness. Story after story in this book brings tears to my eyes and goosebumps to my skin, and frees a steady aching in my weary heart. For all that we do wrong as human beings, to each other and to the earth, we do one thing that cannot ever be wrong, again and again: we practice kindness.

I'm thinking about the story of the hiker left for dead on Mt. Everest, who repays the Sherpa village that saved him by moving there and joining their community. A little money, a gift of three apples, or spiritual comfort coming at the moment it is most desperately needed. A reciprocal, blossoming kindness, like the man who ran two blocks to check on his neighbor lying on the ground, who he assumed was hurt, or worse. When he got there and found the neighbor was just resting, he lay down next to him in the grass, and got the glorious gift of looking up at the beautiful sky for the first time in a long while. A contagious kindness, like the destitute Haitian boy who was given two shirts, and cheerfully passed one on to a friend.

Kindness is gratitude turned to action. Kindness is love made manifest.

The wonderful playwright Sarah Ruhl's young daughter asked her, "Why make theater?" And she responded, "Because it is fun. Because it is ancient. Because it is radically tangible and accessible in the digital age. Because it makes you feel like a child." I say the same is true of kindness. It is fun, and hyper-rewarding—getting is great, giving is even better. It is ancient, and part of our very makeup. We know this for sure because of stories and fables and songs and plays passed down. But even more so, we know it because, well, we still exist. And without kindness of any kind that would be a long shot. Kindness is here for the taking. Anyone can do it, at any time. You can do it right now. You don't even have to get up. Your kind thoughts move inner mountains, and all the better when they lead to kind actions of any sort—simple, quiet, quick, outrageous, impossible, steadying, heartening, anything!

And kindness, like theatre, makes you feel like a child. Use your imagination, enter a space with a bold plan, see a need and fulfill it. Bring along your toolkit of laughter, bright eyes, open heart, new tricks, and old skills that lie dormant, waiting to launch their heft against some pain or problem.

My optimism for this collapsing world rests on two thoughts. First, we humans are tool users, inventors, and ingenious problem solvers. The speed and connection of our world has brought new challenges, sure, but also incredible reach and collaboration. We have a whole new ability to quickly focus our ingenuity to a laser point, and really get things done. We can focus our kindness in the same way. In addition, each random act of kindness is also an act of invention, and, whether planned in advance or spontaneous, each one is a little self-propelled machine of trust and love, sent off to do its business in the world.

Second, kindness is the child of love. And love is expansive. That's how you know it's love. It cannot be stopped in its growth and reach, even when the walls are closing in. Love and kindness move the human story forward.

In this book I am reminded of the power of kindness in story after story—through enormous vulnerability and caring response, through acts of generosity that are random to the giver but deliberate and perfect in the eyes of the getter. How important books like this are, and what a profound effect this one has on my everyday life, each time I read it: I am inspired to do something kind, today, tomorrow, and the next day. I am spurred into grateful memory of all the simple, loving, generous things done by those around me.

In a world of diminishing resources, the well of kindness is infinite, and self-replenishing. It is local and global at the same time. We can feel it, see it, know it, remember it, share it, tell stories about it, and pass it on. It is human. It is ours for the taking, and, most importantly, ours for the giving.

—Addie Johnson
Summer 2012

Acknowledgments

Gratitudes to all who have contributed their stories to our Random Acts of Kindness books. Know that you have helped inspire a kindness revolution. Long may it flourish.

To Our Readers

Conari Press, an imprint of Red Wheel/Weiser, publishes books on topics ranging from spirituality, personal growth, and relationships to women's issues, parenting, and social issues. Our mission is to publish quality books that will make a difference in people's lives—how we feel about ourselves and how we relate to one another. We value integrity, compassion, and receptivity, both in the books we publish and in the way we do business.

Our readers are our most important resource, and we appreciate your input, suggestions, and ideas about what you would like to see published.

Visit our website at *www.redwheelweiser.com* to learn about our upcoming books and free downloads, and be sure to go to *www.redwheelweiser.com/newsletter/* to sign up for newsletters and exclusive offers.

You can also contact us at *info@redwheelweiser.com*.

Conari Press
an imprint of Red Wheel/Weiser, LLC
665 Third Street, Suite 400
San Francisco, CA 94107